The relationship of faith and works is one of the most important and yet disputed topics in the history of the church. In this book, Chris Bruno, who is a careful biblical scholar with a heart for the church, dismantles the false dichotomy between believing in justification by faith alone and being zealous for good works. I hope many read this book and learn the profound and yet practical truth that we are saved by faith alone but that saving faith never remains alone. Real faith produces good works.

Jeremy Treat
Pastor for preaching and vision at Reality LA
Adjunct professor of theology at Biola University
Author of *Seek First* and *The Crucified King*

Chris uses a conversational format to walk through background information and current scholastic thought on the issues surround James and Paul's alleged conflict on works and faith. In an easy to understand fashion, Chris explains the Paul and James don't conflict, but complement each other, more fully explaining both sides of the coin.

Mark Lanier
Author, *Christianity on Trial*
Lawyer and Bible teacher

Chris Bruno tackles the perennial yet parochially Protestant problem of aligning the apostle Paul and James the Just when it comes to faith and works. What Bruno shows is that if the letter of James is an epistle of straw, then Paul's letter to the Galatians too is stuffed with straw. Through a meticulous description of the life and context of Paul and James and a concerted comparison of their respective letters, Bruno succeeds in demonstrating how these two pillars of the church are really singing off the same sheet of gospel music.

Michael F. Bird
Academic Dean and Lecturer in Theology at Ridley College in Melbourne, Australia

Chris Bruno he has shown in this very accessible but profound book that James and Paul cohere in their theology of justification. Bruno demonstrates that faith and works in both Paul and James are not enemies but friends, but at the same time he carefully explains what Paul and James mean by the key terms faith, works, and justification. I am confident that many will come to a clear understanding of how Paul and James fit together by reading this work.

Thomas Schreiner

Professor of New Testament Interpretation at the Southern Baptist Theological Seminary

In *Paul vs. James*, Chris Bruno gives readers an engaging, faithful, and practical way to understand what is often portrayed as a major source of tension in the New Testament. Instead of seeing conflict between how Paul and James understand justification and the relationship between faith and works, Bruno argues that there is exegetical, canonical, and theological unity in what they say about this vital topic. This is an excellent introduction to the debate and to a way forward in it that retains historically orthodox and Protestant commitments.

Matthew Y. Emerson

Dickinson Associate Professor of Religion
Director, Master of Arts in Christian Studies and Intercultural Studies Programs
Hobbs College of Theology and Ministry

Many pit the Old Testament against the New, the Gospels against Paul, and James against Paul. Bruno argues that the two apostles, in reality, reinforce each other. The brilliance of this book lies in its accessibility and wholistic understanding of Paul and James. This project will serve the church well in its informed theology, responsible handling of biblical texts, and application for today. Well done.

Benjamin L. Gladd

Associate Professor of New Testament
Reformed Theological Seminary, Jackson, MS

PAUL

WHAT WE'VE BEEN MISSING IN THE FAITH AND WORKS DEBATE

VS.

CHRIS BRUNO

JAMES

MOODY PUBLISHERS
CHICAGO

Edited by Kevin P. Emmert
Interior Design: Ragont Design
Cover Design: Faceout Studio
Cover portrait of St. Paul copyright © 2018 by alexsol / Shutterstock (83480905).
Cover portrait of St. James is in the public domain.
Cover background paper texture copyright © 2018 by Ensuper / Shutterstock (68245945).
Cover background paper texture copyright © 2018 by M.E. Mulder / Shutterstock (25320586).
Cover background paper texture copyright © 2018 by HABRDA / Shutterstock (69847345).
Cover background paper texture copyright © 2018 by R-studio / Shutterstock (77937742).
All rights reserved for all of the above photos.

All websites and phone numbers listed herein are accurate at the time of publication but may change in the future or cease to exist. The listing of website references and resources does not imply publisher endorsement of the site's entire contents. Groups and organizations are listed for informational purposes, and listing does not imply publisher endorsement of their activities.

ISBN: 978-0-8024-1912-5

We hope you enjoy this book from Moody Publishers. Our goal is to provide high-quality, thought-provoking books and products that connect truth to your real needs and challenges. For more information on other books and products written and produced from a biblical perspective, go to www.moodypublishers.com or write to:

Moody Publishers
820 N. LaSalle Boulevard
Chicago, IL 60610

1 3 5 7 9 10 8 6 4 2

Printed in the United States of America

CONTENTS

To
Jonathan Arnold
Scott Dunford
David Griffiths
Heath Hale
Todd Morikawa
Daniel Patz
Thank you for pushing me toward faithful works.

FOREWORD

I n a sermon I heard as a seminary student over forty years ago, the great British preacher John R. W. Stott advocated for what we called "BBC": Balanced, Biblical Christianity. He warned us that one of the quickest routes to heresy in our ministries was imbalance. Not many of us, he noted, were in danger of denying a key biblical truth—we weren't about to teach that Jesus was not divine or that there was no day of judgment to come. But we were in danger of stressing one side of biblical truth so strongly that the other side of the truth got lost—like warning people so often and so insistently about final judgment that they forgot that God's Spirit was active in their lives to keep them in their faith.

Faith and works is one of those issues that is especially hard to keep in balance. In fact, it is easy to identify many occasions in Christian history when this balance has been lost—and to the great harm of the church. Christians in one era might be so anxious to guard "by faith alone" that they neglect the works that God calls us to exhibit. In another time and place, other believers might stress the importance of being disciples of Christ so strongly that they think their good works will earn their way to heaven. Keeping our balance on this issue is particularly hard because the Bible itself seems to say different things. Consider these two verses:

> For we hold that one is justified by faith apart from works
> of the law. (Rom. 3:28)

> You see that a person is justified by works and not by
> faith alone. (James 2:24)

So which is it? Am I put right with God by my faith apart from works (Romans)? Or am I put right before God by a mix of faith and works (James)? A pretty important question!

And so I welcome Chris Bruno's readable and thoroughly biblical exploration of this issue. He sets the matter in both its wider biblical context at the same time as he makes clear its relevance and importance to faithful Christian living today. Most importantly, he demonstrates how a right reading of the Bible reveals that it speaks ultimately with one voice on this issue—helping us to maintain "BBC."

Douglas J. Moo
Kenneth T. Wessner Professor of New Testament

IRRECONCILABLE DIFFERENCES?

What does the Bible really teach about faith and works?

Maybe you've been in a Bible study with a friend who seems to know the Bible well, and you were surprised to hear him say, "Since we are saved by faith, there is nothing left for you to do. In fact, trying to do good only leads to legalism."

Or you might have a neighbor who attends church every time the doors are open. If anyone is a faithful Christian, it has to be her. She recently told you, "We can't expect God to accept us if we are not doing something for Him. God helps those who help themselves."

If you have your biblical wits about you, when you hear ideas like these, you can smell something fishy. But when we actually find ourselves in the middle of one of these conversations, we might not know how to respond.

When we read verses like Romans 3:28 ("one is justified by faith apart from works of the law"), some people respond like the man in the Bible study. They might say if we ever try to do anything good to please God, then we are in danger of legalism and self-righteousness. But that doesn't quite square with the many places in the New Testament wherein we are actually commanded to do something.

Other people might be more inclined to focus on all of those commands to obey. When they read a verse like James 2:24 ("a person is justified by works and not by faith alone") they end up like the church-lady neighbor, basically trying to work their way to heaven. But that doesn't seem to fit either.

My guess is that if you're reading this book, you take the whole Bible seriously and won't end up at either of these extremes. Or at least you won't say these kinds of things out loud. But if we're being honest, we often end up leaning toward one of these positions.

You might not come right out and say that works don't matter, but when you talk to your kids or people in your church about what it means to follow Jesus, you never talk about obedience. Instead, you emphasize making a decision, praying a prayer, or signing a card. Saving faith begins and ends in a single moment. While good works are the icing on the cake, you can still have the cake without the icing.

Or maybe you say just the opposite. Following Jesus is not simply about what you believe, but about what you *do*. What really matters when it comes to following Jesus is that you care for the "least of these." Those who are loose on their doctrine yet feed the hungry, give to the poor, and promote human flourishing are more Christian than those who hold firm to the "truth" but don't care about these good works.

If you find yourself sympathizing with one of these perspectives, then this book is for you.

An Epistle of Straw?

But maybe you don't see yourself in either of these extremes. You understand the Bible teaches that we are saved by faith alone but that true saving faith never remains alone. It produces good works. You know that Paul's teaching on justification by faith and James's emphasis on works fit together somehow, but you still can't quite articulate how.

You might know a college freshman sitting in her Introduction to Religion course at a local state university who heard her professor claim, "The Bible is full of contradictions. Paul says we are saved by faith through grace, not by works. James says justification is by works and not by faith alone." When she comes to you asking for an answer, you can talk her down from the existential ledge, but you can tell she's not quite satisfied with your answer.

If you're a student of church history, you may know that Martin Luther made some confusing statements about the Epistle of James. He called it "an epistle of straw" that "has nothing of the nature of the gospel about it,"[1] and also wrote that James "mangles the Scriptures and thereby opposes Paul and all Scripture."[2] *Et tu*, Brother Martin? How is a good Protestant to respond when they hear Martin Luther apparently teaming up with the ungodly college professor to attack the unity of Scripture?

When most Christians hear these sorts of claims, they instinctively know otherwise. We usually recognize the great contribution to the canon that James makes and are edified by his exhortations on wisdom, the tongue, caring for the poor, prayer, and faith. At the same time, many Christians, even many evangelical pastors, can't help but squirm a little in their seats when they hear James say that "a person is justified by works and not by faith alone."

And when some of these pastors hear unbelieving scholars discuss the extreme diversity in the early church, they know something isn't quite right. But when they hear these experts talking about how James and Paul represent contradictory

"Jewish Christianity" and "Gentile Christianity," they aren't sure how to answer. And they aren't quite sure how they would answer if one of their church members asked questions about the varieties of early Christianity—or "Christianities."

If you find yourself nodding your head at any of these scenarios, then this book is also for you.

The Way Forward

In the pages that follow, we will journey through the lives and teachings of James and Paul to see whether they really disagreed about justification and other related issues. In order to understand what these apostles taught and why they taught it, we will step back and consider their lives, callings, and mission as important contexts for their teaching. Along the way, we'll correct our misunderstandings of justification and good works and clarify how we ought to respond to others who misrepresent the relationship between James and Paul on this and other issues.

As we begin this journey, we need to remember that the New Testament was not written in a sterile seminary classroom. Paul, James, and the rest of the authors of the New Testament were not writing clinical instruction manuals. Instead, they were writing field-survival guides while they were in the field! As we understand their backgrounds and the shared message and mission of James and Paul, we might be surprised to find how close these men were. They had a shared commitment to reaching the entire Roman Empire, the entire world, with the gospel of Jesus Christ. And at times, they worked closely together to devise a strategy for this mission.[3]

After we've seen the unity of James and Paul in their message and mission, we'll turn our attention to their own teachings on justification in part 2. Before we get to their letters, we'll start in the Old Testament, because both James and Paul build their understanding of justification from the story of Abraham and especially the proclamation of Abraham's faith in Genesis 15:6. When we see how they both read and apply this text, we may be surprised again to see their remarkable unity on justification and good works.

James and Paul are fighting the same battle defending the gospel, standing back-to-back fending off enemies on both sides. James is fighting against a false faith that denies good works are the necessary fruit of saving faith. When we swivel around to Paul, we see he is battling a wrong understanding of good works that fails to see faith in Christ as the only ground for our acceptance before God.

In the last part of the book, we'll apply these truths in our lives and churches. We'll summarize what James and Paul teach us about faith and works, and learn from others throughout church history who have asked some of the same questions that we will discuss. Finally, we'll examine how we should teach and preach on faith and works today and what James and Paul might have to say to some pressing pastoral questions we often face. A misunderstanding of faith or works could have tragic consequences. To misunderstand the New Testament's unified teaching on faith, works, and justification will minimize the seriousness of sin, the transforming power of the gospel, and the very nature of our hope in Christ. This is no light matter.

As I've studied, read, and taught about the relationship between Paul and James and the interplay between faith and works in different settings over the years, I've found that many Bible-believing Christians subtly buy into one of the false perspectives we described above. But as I've dug into the Scriptures to correct these misunderstandings—beginning with my own!—I've seen people grow in their confidence in the Scriptures as they understand and learn to apply to their lives the important inter-play between faith and works. As we walk through this study, I pray that we come to understand better what it means to follow Jesus faithfully.

In His great wisdom, God gave us both Paul's epistles and the epistle of James. We ignore one or both of these to our great loss. But as we learn to read these letters as part of the glori-ous, unified teaching about justification, faith, and works, we will walk away with a stronger confidence in the unity of God's revelation in the whole Bible, greater faith in God's promises, and a deeper hope in the transforming work of the Spirit. Isn't that what we are after?

Let's not waste any more time. Travel with me to first-century Galilee, to the home of Joseph, the carpenter, father of Jesus and His brother James.

PART 1

The Lives
of James and Paul

Chapter 1

JAMES, BROTHER OF JESUS

We know a lot more about Paul's early life than we do about James's. Paul wrote thirteen letters in the New Testament, and most of them have biographical tidbits peppered throughout. Paul also dominates the second half of the book of Acts, so we have a lot of information from him and about him in the New Testament.

The material on James, on the other hand, is a little spotty. Yes, he is a prominent figure in Acts, but Peter and Paul tend to dominate the narrative in that book. We have one letter from him, but it includes almost nothing in the way of biographical detail. In fact, we get more details about James from Paul's letters than we do from James himself! In Galatians 1, Paul calls James "the Lord's brother" (v. 19), along with some other details that we'll come back to later.[1] The Gospels also include James in the list of Jesus' brothers. When the people in Nazareth were shocked by Jesus' teaching, they ask, "Is not this the carpenter, the son of Mary and brother of James and Joses and Judas and Simon? And are not his sisters here with us?" (Mark 6:3; see also Matt. 13:55).

The first thing to know about James's upbringing and early life is that he is called the "the Lord's brother." If we have Protestant ears, what this means is pretty straightforward. James was the son of Mary and Joseph, so he was Jesus' brother. Roman Catholics believe that James and other men and women that the Gospels call Jesus' brothers and sisters were actually His close relatives, not His biological siblings. Part of this question is related to a debate about whether Mary remained a perpetual virgin, and this chapter is about James, not Mary, so we can't linger on this question.

If we are going to be fair, we also have to admit that even many well-known Protestant Reformers like Martin Luther, Ulrich Zwingli, and Thomas Cranmer also believed in Mary's lifelong virginity. However, this question was debated by the earliest Christians, and Matthew 1:25 says that Joseph and Mary did not have sexual intercourse "until" she gave birth to Jesus. This implies that they had a normal marriage that included sex and procreation after Jesus was born. I know my Roman Catholic friends have certain reasons for what they believe about Mary, but this belief could make Jesus' humanity and birth almost docetic (Docetism is the heresy that Jesus only seemed to be human, but really was not). If Jesus' birth did not have the normal effects on Mary's body, then it only seemed to be a normal human birth. And that might lead us to an unbiblical view of Jesus and the gospel. The truth is, whether James was Jesus' brother, cousin, uncle, or some other relative does not change most of the conclusions we'll reach here. Regardless of how exactly they were related, the consistent witness of the New Testament is that James was part of Jesus' family, so it is clear that James grew up in the village of Nazareth in Galilee.

Galilee of the Gentiles

Even though we don't have the same amount of evidence about Galilee as we do about Jerusalem around the same time, that doesn't mean we don't know anything about it. To get a handle on what Nazareth was like in the first century, we need to step back a few centuries to Israel's exile in Babylon and Assyria. After centuries of rebellion against God's rule over them, He sent Israel in the north and, later, Judah in the south into exile. Their enemies in Assyria (Israel) and Babylon (Judah) invaded them and carried away their leading citizens. The promised land was under the authority of foreign rulers.

Without their leaders in power and without the temple in operation during the exile, many of the Jews who were still in the land intermarried with the surrounding nations. The descendants of these intermarriages were the Samaritans, whom we hear about in the Gospels. By the time James was growing up, the Romans had divided the land into several provinces: Judea in the south, Galilee in the north, and Samaria between them (the structure and borders shifted as different foreign rulers came and went, but we'll focus on just those three).

With the region of the Samaritans lying between them and Jerusalem and the rebuilt temple, Galilee was often seen as something of a backwater region. On top of that, Nazareth, a small village in Galilee, was kind of a backwater in a backwater.

Even though it was far from Jerusalem, many fervent Jews who lived in Galilee were devoted to worshiping in the temple and keeping the Law. We know that Jesus' family was devout. Mary's relatives, Elizabeth and Zechariah, the parents of John the Baptist, served in the temple in Jerusalem. Mary and Joseph also had a fervent faith in God, and they were devoted to keeping the Law. At least once a year, they would travel to Jerusalem for the Passover. This is why they were in Jerusalem when Jesus stayed behind in the temple (Luke 2:41–52). He was not trained as a rabbi or Pharisee the way that Paul later was, but we can say with confidence that James grew up learning the Scriptures and being devoted to following the God of Israel.

Also, James likely learned the same carpentry trade that

Joseph and Jesus did (Mark 6:3), and this trade probably included several different types of construction work. If so, then he would have interacted with Gentiles regularly in the larger nearby town of Sepphoris, which was about three miles from Nazareth. Sepphoris probably had a largely Jewish population, but throughout the first century, it also had a growing Roman influence and was becoming more and more Hellenized (influenced by Greek language and culture). Even though it isn't mentioned in the Gospels (a detail that may be telling in itself), it would have been impossible to avoid an occasional visit to this larger town and to interact with the Gentiles there.

To sum up, James and Jesus grew up in a family and home that was seriously devoted to the Law while living in a region that had a number of Greco-Roman influences, so they likely learned Greek in their early years. They also grew up far from the leaders of the Jews and the governing authorities in Jerusalem. Not many Jews in the first century would've expected the Messiah, the king who would reestablish the throne of David, to grow up there. As Nathanael asked Philip when he heard about Jesus, "Can anything good come out of Nazareth?" (John 1:46). Just about everyone living in Judea in the first century would have answered no. When James was growing up, being a leader in Jerusalem was probably the furthest thing from his mind. Yet this does not mean that he would have been anything less than a fervent and loyal Jew, striving to keep the Law and eagerly waiting for the Messiah to come. And during the earthly ministry of Jesus, James saw his brother as anything but the Messiah he expected.

Not Even His Brothers Believed in Him

I imagine it was difficult growing up with Jesus as your brother. Imagine if you had a sibling who never sinned. And He was born after an angel visited your mother and father to tell them about His miraculous birth. The Gospels don't tell us anything about the dynamics of growing up with Jesus as one's brother, but it had to be difficult at times.

John 7:5 tells us that His brothers did not believe in Him during His ministry before the resurrection, but the first time we hear about His brothers is in the episode recorded in Matthew 12:46–50 (with parallels in Mark 3:31–35 and Luke 8:19–21). As the crowds around Him increased, His mother and brothers had trouble accessing him. Jesus' answer probably didn't win Him many style points in their eyes: "Whoever does the will of my Father in heaven is my brother and sister and mother" (v. 50). James may have just rolled his eyes or he may have been angry at what he saw as a slight to Mary. Some scholars have suggested that they were following John the Baptist. Given the family in which they grew up, I think this is possible, maybe even likely. In any case, James did not believe in Jesus during His earthly life. This does not mean, however, that James and his brothers were not interested in keeping the Law or following the God of Israel. In fact, one historical tradition says that James was a Nazarite who took special vows to devote himself to prayer and purity.[2]

We hear about Jesus' brothers again in the next chapter in Matthew (Matt. 13:53–58; see also Mark 6:1–6). When Jesus returned to Nazareth to preach in the synagogue after teaching in many nearby villages, His close family and friends were astonished. They knew Him growing up and surely saw that He was a unique boy, but they did not expect anything like the wisdom He showed in His teaching or the power He displayed in His miracles (v. 54). They knew His mother Mary and His brothers—James, Joses, Simon, and Judas. Since their father, Joseph, was not mentioned, it is most likely that he had died sometime before then. They took offense at Jesus and did not believe in Him (vv. 57–58).

In John 2, we get a fleeting glimpse at Jesus' brothers and Mary when He stayed with them in Capernaum (John 2:12). Then John 7 is the only place we hear Jesus' brothers speak, when they asked Him to go to Judea for the Feast of Booths. They told Him that He should not keep His works a secret but instead, "show yourself to the world" (v. 4).

Their motive, however, was not to increase His ministry. In fact, they asked Him this because they did not yet believe in Him (v. 5). They wanted more evidence before they would believe in Him. Or maybe they wanted Jesus to be exposed as a fraud so that He would return home and stop shaming the family. Either way, they were not asking Him to come to Judea out of good motives, and they were not with Him through His trial and execution (notice their apparent absence in John 19:25–27). Even if they were followers of John the Baptist before Jesus was crucified, Jesus' brothers did not believe He was the Messiah or that He was doing God's will. Like another young Jewish man who grew up in Tarsus, they wanted to follow the God of Israel but did not at first believe that Jesus was really the Messiah. Then, after Jesus' execution, everything changed.

Chapter 2

PAUL, PERSECUTOR OF THE CHURCH

About twenty years before Jesus' crucifixion, a few hundred miles northwest of Galilee in modern-day Turkey, a Jewish boy named Saul was born in Tarsus. This boy would grow up to be the man we know now as St. Paul. But, by his own testimony, he didn't exactly begin life as a saint. In this chapter, we want to put together as much as we can about Saul's early life until his calling and conversion on the road to Damascus.

Paul or Saul?

Before we start walking through what we can know of Paul's upbringing, let's straighten out the confusion about his name. Contrary to what many of us learned in Sunday school, nowhere in the Bible are we told that Saul changed his name to Paul after he started following Jesus. In fact, he is called "Saul" several times in Acts 13, which takes place years after he was converted (13:1, 7, 9). If he left behind that name when he was converted, someone didn't get the memo. Some scholars think that he took the name "Paul" in honor of Sergius Paulus, a Roman official on

Cyprus who began to follow Jesus after hearing Paul's preaching (Acts 13:12). This is possible, but I think there is a simpler explanation for the different names.

Every Roman citizen was given three names. Think of them like your first, middle, and last name. If his father was a Roman citizen who was also a devout Jew, it would make sense that Paul would have a Greco-Roman name (*Paulos*) and a Jewish name (*Saulos*). It is likely that "Paul" and "Saul" were two of his three names (we don't know exactly what order they came in or what the third name was). It would make most sense to go by "Saul" when he ministered in a primarily Jewish audience, and when he was on his Gentile mission, "Paul" would fit well.[1] With that out of the way, I'm going to call him "Paul" from here on.

Now back to Tarsus.

Tarsus

In Acts 22:28, Paul says he that was born a Roman citizen, so his father was a citizen as well. We don't know how they got this status, but it was somewhat rare for Jews to be Roman citizens—especially Jews who remained faithful to the Law of Moses. One historical tradition that goes back to Jerome in the fourth century AD speculates that the Romans brought Paul's family to Tarsus from Judea as prisoners of war (maybe when Pompey captured Jerusalem in 63 BC). Later, when Tarsus became the capital of that region, its citizens, including Paul's family, may have been granted citizenship as well.

By the first century, Tarsus was the capital of the Roman province of Cilicia, and later in his life, Paul would call it "no obscure city" (Acts 21:39). It was a "free city," which meant that its citizens weren't taxed by the Roman Empire. This was a little bit like Florida and Texas and other states that don't have state income tax, except in this case there was not "federal," or imperial, tax.

If we look at a map of modern Turkey, Tarsus is in the south-eastern corner of Asia Minor, near the Turkey–Syria border. In the first century, the city was near a major trade route that went from Egypt, Judea, and Syria through Asia Minor, eventually leading to Rome. A lot of trading occurred in and around Tarsus, and it was possible to do well for yourself there with a little hard work and a few opportunities.

Apparently, Paul's family was doing okay, because they were prosperous enough to send him to Jerusalem to receive a high-quality education at the feet of Gamaliel, probably the best-known rabbi in the city during that time. His family may have also sent his siblings there, because we know from Acts 22 and 23 that later in his life, Paul's sister and nephew were living in Jerusalem.

Just like James's, Paul's parents were devout Jews, and they sent their son to Jerusalem to be educated in the Law. But Paul received much more extensive training in the Law and the traditions of the Pharisees than James did. This young man would grow to be a zealous defender of the Law and the developing traditions of the rabbis. But, also like James's, his path was radically redirected in a way he never could have expected.

Education and Upbringing

As a Roman citizen, Paul would have also had access to a Greco-Roman education in Tarsus. We know from places like Acts 17, when Paul debated with the philosophers at the Areopagus in Athens, that he was familiar with Greco-Roman philosophy, and some scholars argue that his letters demonstrate that he knew the basics of Greco-Roman rhetoric. Like Athens, Tarsus was known for its love for philosophy, so Paul would have had access to the Greco-Roman schools in the city.

Somewhere along the way, he also learned a trade. Paul has typically been called a "tentmaker," so much so that we often use this label for anyone who works another job while also working in ministry. However, the word "tentmaker" can be a little bit misleading. Paul was not making North Face–type tents. Instead, the word means something like a leather worker. Leather was usually used to make tents, but he may have made other things as well. Later in life, he used his ability to make a living to help support himself as he traveled throughout the Roman Empire.

In spite of his education in the Greco-Roman world and the trade that he learned from his father, Paul's primary identity was as a follower of the God of Israel, and his primary education was in Jerusalem under Rabbi Gamaliel. As he wrote later in his life, Paul was "a Hebrew of Hebrews" (Phil. 3:5–6). He proudly traced his heritage to the tribe of Benjamin, which had produced another well-known Saul about one thousand years earlier. He was circumcised on the eighth day, according to the Law of Moses, and he was zealous to live by that Law.

As a student of the Law in the first century, Paul would have studied the Old Testament Scriptures at a level that would intimidate even some of the most learned Hebrew scholars in the world today. If the later rabbis are a reliable guide to what his education would have looked like, to become a Pharisee, a title that Paul later claimed for himself, he would have had to memorize most or all of the Old Testament. Given his self-professed zeal for the traditions of his fathers (Gal. 1:14), it is more likely than not that he memorized the whole thing.

I'd love to be able to tell other stories about Paul's upbringing and young adulthood, but we've covered just about everything we know about his early life and education. We don't know if he was ever married, but he was in his midforties and single when he wrote 1 Corinthians around AD 55. It was unusual for a Pharisee or a prominent Jew to be unmarried, but we also see a pretty significant exception to this rule in the life of Jesus. Some have speculated that Paul's wife died or that she left him when he started to follow Jesus. I'm inclined to think that Paul was likely married at some point. But it is also possible that he was so devoted to studying the Torah that he decided a wife would hold him back. Either way, he was single during his apostolic ministry.

When he finished his education, Paul stayed in Jerusalem and became part of the Pharisees. We remember these guys from the Gospels. Many of them passionately sought to obey the Law—at virtually any cost. They learned it, learned how to keep it, and sought to teach others how to keep it. They were passionate to maintain the purity of the nation and to keep the Gentiles from corrupting them.

The only problem was that many of them also misunderstood the purpose of the Law. Many of them thought that the Law was the be-all and end-all of God's revelation to His people, almost as if the Law existed for the sake of the Law and that obedience to the Law would be the path to winning favor with God. The Law became the fence that separated Jew and Gentile and gave Israel a special status above all other nations. This was likely Paul's attitude toward the Law. He was zealous to keep it—and he would not put up with anyone who tried to undermine it, because he saw this as a threat to Israel's salvation and special status.

We also don't know if Paul ever saw Jesus before His death and resurrection. If he was a Pharisee or a Pharisee-in-training during the years of Jesus' public ministry, it is difficult to imagine that he wouldn't have seen or at least heard about Jesus at some point. Either way, Paul himself never mentions seeing Jesus until later, on the road to Damascus.

"Breathing Threats and Murder"

Within a year or two of Jesus' resurrection and ascension, the early Christian movement was gaining momentum in Jerusalem. Thousands of people in Jerusalem had believed in Jesus, were baptized, and became a part of the church. Even though some of the apostles were beaten and thrown in prison, God had delivered them so they could continue preaching and teaching. The final straw for some of the Jewish leaders may have been when many priests believed in Jesus (Acts 6:7). Just after this, as he was proclaiming the good news of Jesus, Stephen, one of the early leaders in the Jerusalem church, was grabbed by the Sanhedrin (the Jewish ruling council). As they listened to his sermon retelling of Israel's history, these men were incensed. The culmination of Israel's story, according to Stephen, was not the Law or the temple. The climax of God's plan for His people was not the restoration of the temple or a group of people who perfectly kept the Law. For Stephen and the other Christians, the culmination of God's plan for His people was the life, death, resurrection, and reign of Jesus, the true Messiah and Savior. And the Jewish rulers had been a part of His execution, just as their fathers had killed the prophets before them (Acts 7:51–53).

For these men, this was blasphemy! The Pharisees saw themselves as Israel's leaders and champions, not its villains. And to attack the place of the Law and the temple was just too much. The men of the Sanhedrin took off their coats, picked up stones, and began throwing them at Stephen. Even as he died, he continued to proclaim Jesus, the true Savior and Messiah.

As they prepared to stone Stephen, the men laid their coats at the feet of Paul. This may even symbolize his authority as one of the key leaders in this group. In any case, he was certainly approving of the action and encouraged it to continue. After

Stephen's martyrdom, Paul moved to a whole new level of persecuting the church. Over the next several months or years, he devoted himself to stamping out the followers of Jesus. Acts tells us that Paul was "ravaging the church" (Acts 8:3) and "breathing threats and murder against the disciples of the Lord" (Acts 9:1). Paul himself wrote that he "persecuted the church of God violently and tried to destroy it" (Gal. 1:13).

Protecting the law and wiping out anyone who undermined it was his self-proclaimed mission from God, so Paul took it upon himself to round up as many Christians as he could find in Jerusalem. He had to stop them from spreading their heresy about a Messiah who rose from the dead and claimed to be greater than the Law itself. When he heard about this message spreading beyond Jerusalem to places like Damascus, he had to go there and stop these heretics. And so, Paul set out for Damascus with official authorization from the high priest in Jerusalem to arrest any followers of Jesus, this pretend Messiah. However, his trip did not go as planned. As he traveled to Damascus, he was confronted by the resurrected Lord Himself.

We can point to many differences in their upbringing and early life, but both James and Paul were raised to follow the Law and to be devoted to the God of Israel. Both rejected Jesus' claim to be the Messiah when they first heard, and both encountered the risen Lord, and their lives were set on a new trajectory.

Chapter 3

JAMES THE JUST, SERVANT OF JESUS CHRIST

Forty days after His resurrection, Jesus ascended to His Father, where He sat down to rule on the throne of David until He returns in power and glory (Eph. 1:20–23). Even though none of the Gospels tell us how James or the other brothers of Jesus had changed their minds about Him, Luke tells us that shortly after Jesus had ascended, the remaining apostles, a group of women, and the brothers of Jesus were all together, "devoting themselves to prayer" (Acts 1:14). They had become followers of their brother, the crucified Messiah.

What in the world had happened? In John 7, Jesus' brothers did not believe in Him. In John 19, during the crucifixion, they were not around—or at least not mentioned. By the time we get to Acts 1, James and the other brothers had joined the followers of Jesus.

The only reasonable answer is that they met the resurrected Messiah. In 1 Corinthians 15:7, Paul says that sometime after His resurrection, Jesus had appeared to James. James either told the rest of his brothers about this or Jesus Himself appeared to all the brothers. Either way, James and the other brothers of Jesus could no longer deny what and who their brother really was and is.

Again, we can only speculate about how they would have responded when they realized that they had been wrong about Jesus, had been wrong to doubt Him, and had been wrong to misunderstand Him so often. I know it is a Christian cliché to make a Narnia comparison, but this is a Christian book, so let's go with it.

In *The Lion, the Witch and the Wardrobe*, Edmund betrays his siblings and all of Narnia to the White Witch. To be fair, he had been enchanted by Turkish Delight and the Witch's magic. To betray your siblings for Turkish Delight, it would have to be enchanted. Have you ever tasted it? It is like road tar with powdered sugar sprinkled on it.

Anyway, when Edmund is finally rescued from the White Witch and meets Aslan, we find Edmund and Aslan walking alone in a field. As C. S. Lewis writes, "There is no need to tell you (and no one ever heard) what Aslan was saying but it was a conversation which Edmund never forgot."[1] I imagine the first meeting James had with the risen Jesus something like this. There is no need for us to know what was said, but it was certainly a conversation that James never forgot. To be sure, James did not betray Jesus the same way that Edmund betrayed his siblings, but there was perhaps a fractured relationship between the brothers that was restored when James finally came to see who Jesus truly is.

When Aslan walked Edmund back to his siblings, he said to them, "Here is your brother . . . there is no need to talk to him about what is past."[2] Again, I imagine Jesus bringing James back to the apostles and saying something similar: "Here is your brother. There is no need to talk to him about what is past." James, and the other brothers of the Lord, had become followers of Jesus.

James in Jerusalem

The next time we see James is in Acts 12, probably about ten or twelve years after the ascension. By this time, he was not only one of the growing number of Jesus followers in Jerusalem, but he was also a recognized leader in the church. Given his close connection to Jesus, this should be expected. If he was the oldest of Jesus' brothers, then it would have been natural for many early Christians to look to him for leadership. Yet he had not just inherited the role of church leader. From everything we see in the New Testament and other early Christian writings, James was a godly man, devoted to prayer. If James was a Nazarite, then he likely continued fasting and praying regularly even after he began following Jesus. The early church historian Eusebius wrote that James "used to enter the Temple alone, and be found resting on his knees and praying for forgiveness for the people, so that his knees became as hard as those of a camel because of his constant bending forward on his knees in worshipping God and begging for forgiveness for the people."[3] In fact, in many Christian traditions, James is known as "James the Just." And as we'll see below, the epistle of James gives us a window into James's clear devotion to Jesus and pursuit of holiness.

As James was growing in both influence and devotion to Jesus, he assumed an increasingly prominent leadership role in the church in Jerusalem. Then King Herod executed the other James (the son of Zebedee, the brother of John, who was one of the apostles during Jesus' earthly ministry) and arrested Simon Peter, planning to kill him next (Acts 12:1–4). While Peter was waiting to be executed, God miraculously delivered him, and he made it safely out of prison to tell a group of Christians who were praying for his release about what God had done for him.

We don't have time for that whole story, but it's important

to notice what Peter tells the crowd who had gathered to hear this story: "Tell these things to James and to the brothers" (Acts 12:17). By this time, James was recognized by Peter and the other Christians as a leader and influential elder in the church in Jerusalem. Also, in his first meeting with Peter that Paul describes in Galatians 1:18–19, he mentions James as the only other apostle that he met, and in the next chapter, he calls him one of the "pillar" apostles in Jerusalem along with Peter and John (Gal. 2:9).

After the other James—who was likely a cousin of Jesus and James—was executed, Peter left Jerusalem to preach in other places in Acts 12, and John doesn't appear in Acts after chapter 8. Like Peter, he was traveling to other places to preach the gospel. That left James as the central leader of the church in Jerusalem, where he stayed for the rest of his life.

For the next several decades, James was not only the most prominent elder in the church in Jerusalem, but also a leader among Jews scattered around the Mediterranean world. We'll talk about this text more later, but in Galatians 2:12, Paul mentions "certain men came from James" who came to Antioch and convinced Peter and the other Jewish Christians to stop eating with Gentiles. Even though they weren't representing James's view, just using his name was enough to give them some clout in Antioch. More than this though, James's influence can be seen clearly in his epistle that he sent to "the twelve tribes in the Dispersion" (James 1:1) to instruct mostly Jewish Christians how to live out their faith in Jesus.

The Letter of James

Of the many themes in James's letter, let's examine just three: God's fulfillment of His end-time promises in Christ, the status of God's Law in light of the fulfillment of these promises, and faithful living based on these promises. Remember that James is passing on and explaining to his readers the teachings of Jesus Himself. Even though James wasn't a follower of Jesus during His earthly ministry, he certainly witnessed Jesus' teaching and miracles. James was also well-acquainted with Peter and many others who followed Jesus before His death and resurrection. Clearly James knew his brother's teachings about life in the kingdom of God, the coming new covenant, and God's mighty power to keep His covenant promises.

James has a strong view of God's sovereign rule over history, so he grounds all of his commands in God's initiative first. God has fulfilled all of His covenant promises through Jesus, and this fulfillment is the basis of everything that follows. Granted, he doesn't use covenant language the way that Hebrews or even Paul does, but in the introduction of his letter, he emphasizes God's sovereign work to keep His promises: "Of his own will he brought us forth by the word of truth, that we should be a kind of firstfruits of his creatures" (James 1:18).

The idea of a "firstfruit" is a way to talk about the beginning of God's fulfillment of His saving promises. Paul uses it in a similar way in 1 Corinthians 15:20–23, but there Jesus Himself is the first firstfruit. The point in both places is that God is fulfilling His end-time promises now. James talks about the same reality in a different way in James 1:21, where the "implanted word" points back to the new-covenant promise that the Law would be written on our hearts. This fulfills God's promise that He would put his Law within the hearts of His new-covenant people (see Jer. 31:33). From the very beginning of his letter, James is basing all of his instructions on the grace of God in keeping His new-covenant promises to His people.

These new-covenant promises, though, are realized only in and through Jesus. After his introduction in chapter 1, James begins his instructions about how we must live as we "hold the faith in our Lord Jesus Christ, the Lord of glory" (James 2:1). The rest of the book stands in the shadow of the imminent return of the Lord Jesus.[4] James then sees God's new-covenant promises launched through the work of Jesus and looks forward to the day when they will be completed when He returns to judge the world (James 5:9).

James also sees the Law and its fulfillment in light of the new covenant's fulfillment. Have you ever looked at the adjectives James uses to describe the Law? He calls it the "perfect law" (1:25), "the law of liberty" (1:25; 2:12), and the "royal law" (2:8). He also talks about the law without an adjective to describe it in 2:9–11. But in that passage, he is talking about *transgressing* the Law. In the places where he talks about the perfect, royal law of liberty, he is talking about our *fulfillment* of the Law. In light of the work of Jesus and the fulfillment of the new covenant, Christians are now able to keep the Law in some way. This is a new law—a law made perfect by Jesus, the royal law of the king Jesus, the law of liberty that belongs to everyone set free from their sin by Jesus.

This understanding of the Law leads naturally to the third emphasis. James calls his audience to live faithful, patient lives of obedience because God's promises have been launched and will be completed through Jesus. Because the new-covenant promises have been established, we can endure suffering and testing (1:2–3, 10–12; 5:7–18). The law written on our hearts gives us the ability to control the tongue (1:26; 3:1–12), to love others (1:27–28; 2:1–13), not to seek our own glory (3:13–18), and to live at peace with each other (4:1–12). Because our King Jesus will return soon to make all things new and satisfy us in every way, we don't need to cling to the riches and security of this world (1:9–11; 5:1–6). Because of God's work in Jesus, we are able to live out our faith by our works (2:14–26). In all of these instructions, James was picking up on and expanding the teachings of Jesus about the kingdom of God present in the church, the new-covenant community, and the presence of the promised King as He sends His Spirit among us.

Faithful Until the End

James most likely wrote this letter in the late 40s AD. He lived in Jerusalem for another fifteen years or so, teaching about the fulfillment of God's promises through Jesus and how we ought to respond in loyalty to Him. During this time, he and the other apostles grappled with the role of Gentiles in God's new-covenant people, especially as Paul advanced the gospel further west toward Rome. For the rest of his life, James's ministry was focused on Christian Jews in Jerusalem who were turning to follow his crucified and resurrected brother, the Messiah Jesus.

Around AD 62, James was martyred by the Jewish rulers. Eusebius wrote of James's continued influence among the Jews. Many of the leaders came to faith in Jesus, and because of this, some of the scribes and Pharisees wanted to stone him, as they did Stephen. As they began to hurl the stones at him, James, like his brother and Lord, cried out, "Lord, God and Father, forgive them, for they know not what they do."[5] In his death, James was echoing the words of his brother from the cross. As he continued praying for his murderers, one of them hit him with a club on the head to kill him. While we can't be sure about the details, we can have reasonable confidence that, like the Lord Jesus—and, as we will see soon, like Paul—James was murdered for the sake of his faithful proclamation of the gospel, which he continued until the very end of his life.

Chapter 4

PAUL, APOSTLE OF JESUS

When in college, I heard about a friend who met Jim Carrey at an airport and shared the gospel with him. This was in the late 1990s, when Carrey was one of the biggest movie stars and comedians in the world. When I heard that Jim Carrey of all people had heard the gospel, I started praying for him regularly—at least for a few months. I remember saying to another friend something like, "Can you imagine the impact it will have if Jim Carrey becomes a Christian?" Like many other Christians both then and now, I thought that if only this movie star became a Christian, then that would somehow validate the gospel in the eyes of the world.

I think this desire to see famous celebrities—especially movie stars and athletes—come to faith has good intentions, but it is wrong on many levels, not least of which is that God said He typically uses the weak things of the world, not the super-stars (1 Cor. 1:26–29). We often think we are following a biblical precedent: the conversion of Paul, the most famous persecutor of the church. We tend to see this conversion as a paradigm for us, praying that our celebrity of choice might have a "Damascus Road" experience. These kinds of prayers misunderstand not only the way God typically works today, but also Paul's conversion and call on the road to Damascus.

On the Road to Damascus

When we left Paul, he was on his way to Damascus, where he intended to arrest as many Christians as he could and bring them back to Jerusalem for trial. But this trip turned out much differently than he had imagined. As he traveled to Damascus, Paul came face-to-face with the risen Christ.

Imagine how shocking that moment would have been. Paul spent years learning the Scriptures, memorizing the Law, and agonizing over keeping it. He heard about this upstart Christ-following movement that was proclaiming a suffering and risen Messiah. He devoted himself to stamping out this movement and its blasphemy, and he thought that he was serving God by doing this. Then, literally out of the clear blue sky, he was standing face-to-face with this risen Messiah, Jesus.

As he traveled on the road, a light suddenly shone around Paul, and he fell to his knees. Jesus then informed Paul that when he persecuted the church, he was actually persecuting Jesus Himself (Acts 9:5). Because his zeal to serve God was misguided, he ended up opposing the very God he claimed to serve. (Next time we say that all that matters is whether someone is sincere, let's remember that Paul was as sincere as they come, but he was still persecuting Jesus!)

In Acts, Paul tells the story of his conversion three times. In each retelling, he includes more details that clarify what Jesus had told him. By the time we reach the third account in Acts 26:14–28, we've discovered that Jesus revealed to Paul that he was going to proclaim the gospel to the Gentile nations (vv. 17–18). This Pharisee, committed to the purity of the nation, would be sent to proclaim the good news to the Gentiles. In this unique moment in the history of salvation, God called a Pharisee who was doing everything he could to oppose the church of Jesus and to keep the people of God pure from the contamination of the Gentiles. Then Jesus commanded Paul to preach the good news to those same Gentiles.

We can learn something from this account about the way God works to call His people, but I don't think it's helpful to expect every conversion to look like Paul's. God had called this first-century Pharisee to a unique mission as the gospel advanced to the Gentile nations for the first time. If we see Paul's call as the typical Christian experience, then we will lose sight of the uniqueness of what God was doing by calling Paul, rather than James, Peter, or John, to this mission. Understanding the uniqueness of Paul's call helps us better understand his mission to the Gentiles and the background of his teaching on faith and works.

Some scholars debate whether we can properly call Paul's experience a conversion or not. It's true that the lines between Christianity and Judaism were not clearly drawn at the time the way they are today, so we cannot say that Paul was converted from Judaism to Christianity. Remember, the Messiah Jesus was the fulfillment of Israel's hope in the Old Testament. We can say without a doubt that Paul was converted from one way of seeing his relationship with God and His people to a radically different way. No longer did he see his obedience to the Torah and violent commitment to keep himself and others pure as the path to pleasing God. That sure sounds to me like something had changed for Paul, and we might even say he had a conversion.

After their surprising meeting on the road to Damascus, Jesus sent Paul on to the city, where he arrived broken and blind. A Christian named Ananias met him and laid hands on him so that Paul received the gift of the Holy Spirit. He was then baptized and quickly folded into the life of the church in Damascus. The same man who had planned to do everything in his power to end the church just a few days earlier was now a part of it.

Early Days in the Church

After he was baptized in Damascus, Paul traveled to Arabia and then again to Damascus (Gal. 1:17).[1] When he returned to Damascus, there was a plot to kill him, but he escaped in a basket let down outside city walls (Acts 9:23–25). Neither Acts nor Paul's letters tell us what he was doing in Arabia, but we have a clue in one of his later letters. In 2 Corinthians 11, Paul says that he escaped from Damascus because King Aretas was trying to arrest him (2 Cor. 11:32). We know from other sources that King Aretas was the king of the Nabatean kingdom in the northern part of the Arabian Peninsula. Do you see how these pieces might fit together? The king from northern Arabia was trying to arrest Paul after he returned from a season in Arabia. Based on what we know about the rest of his life, what was Paul typically arrested for doing?

Most likely, from the early days of his Christian life, Paul was proclaiming the gospel—in Damascus, in Arabia (Nabataea), and everywhere else he went. Because of this, the Jews and the Nabateans colluded to arrest him, but he slipped through their fingers and went back to Jerusalem.

Paul's visit to Jerusalem was about three years after his conversion, and it was his first time back to the city since he had left to go drag Christians back from Damascus (Gal. 1:18). Unsurprisingly, the Christians in Jerusalem were a little skeptical of Paul. After all, this is the guy who "persecuted the church of God violently and tried to destroy it" (Gal. 1:13). However, the apostles trusted Barnabas, and he intervened to vouch for Paul. After Barnabas saved the day, Paul stayed with Peter for about fourteen days and, as we saw earlier, met James for the first time (Gal. 1:18–19). We'll save the details of this meeting for later. From there, the church in Jerusalem sent him back to Tarsus, possibly because the Jewish leaders who still opposed the Christians had caught wind that the traitor Paul was back in the city.

We don't know much about Paul's life from his return to Tarsus around AD 37 until the beginning of his first "missionary journey" around AD 46. He was near his family, supporting himself with his leather-working, living a faithful Christian life, and certainly proclaiming the good news to everyone around him.

Mission to the West

We'll be somewhat brief in our flyover of the rest of Paul's life, because there has been a lot written about Paul's missionary journeys and ministry.[2] Also, I'm afraid if we go too far down that particular rabbit hole, we may not find the way back out again. We'll have to leave out various details, but I want to remind us of a basic overview of the rest of Paul's life. He suffered in many ways through his life. He was persecuted and shipwrecked and stoned (2 Cor. 11:23–27). He had a lifelong disability of some sort that God used to make him more dependent on Him (2 Cor. 12:7–10). In the midst of all these trials, Paul continued to faithfully labor for the sake of the gospel.

After Paul had been in Tarsus for almost a decade, his friend Barnabas traveled there to bring him back to Antioch, where he quickly became a teacher in the church (Acts 13:1). From there, the Holy Spirit sent Paul and Barnabas on a mission to Cyprus and southeastern Asia Minor. And the rest, as they say, is history. Over the next two decades, Paul traveled through much of the Mediterranean world, proclaiming the gospel to Jews and Gentiles alike, establishing churches, and ordaining elders to lead those churches.

As he preached the gospel among the Gentiles, the church began to wrestle with how these Gentile converts should relate to the mostly Jewish church. Before his conversion, Paul had devoted his life to keeping Israel distinct from the Gentiles. Many Jews continued to hold tightly to these distinctions, including some Jewish Christians. But there was a problem. As Gentiles believed and were baptized, they received the Holy Spirit without being circumcised and becoming full citizens of Israel.

In the Old Testament, any Gentile convert who wanted to become part of the people of God had to be circumcised and keep the Law (Ex. 12:48–49). In the new-covenant people of God, things were different. Gentiles were receiving the gift of the Holy Spirit, which had been promised as part of Israel's restoration. Sorting out this question led to the second meeting of Paul and James, which we'll also talk about in more detail later. For now, we can say that they both saw that God was saving Gentiles as Gentiles, without them having to become part of Israel. The gospel was going to the nations!

The Letters of Paul

While Paul stayed connected to the apostles in Jerusalem in different ways, he spent most of the rest of his life taking the gospel further and further west. As he traveled, preached, worked, and served the growing church, Paul started writing letters to the churches that he had established, to leaders in those churches, and even to other churches he planned to visit soon. Thirteen of those letters were inspired by God as authoritative Scripture and have ended up in our New Testament.

Like the epistle of James, we could write many books about Paul's theological emphases in these letters—and trust me, many books have been written. I want us to consider the same three emphases that we saw in James's epistle. Obviously, we have a lot more material to work with from Paul's thirteen letters than we did from James's one letter. But as we think about the fulfillment of God's promises, the Old Testament Law, and the nature of Christian obedience in this new era, we'll see that even when they are playing a different melody, Paul and James often hit the same notes. We can see these themes in many places in Paul's letters, but we'll stick mainly to Romans, Galatians, and 1 and 2 Corinthians here.

Like James, Paul sees the sovereign power of God on display in His new-covenant promises. In 2 Corinthians 3, Paul is explaining and defending his status as a minister of the new covenant, and he too alludes to God's promises from Jeremiah 31. He calls the Corinthian church a "letter" because the tablet of their heart has been written on with the "ink" of the Spirit (2 Cor. 3:3). In other words, Christians in Corinth were now experiencing the promises of the new covenant. God had replaced their hearts of stone with hearts of flesh and wrote the law on their hearts. Paul goes on to speak of the amazing glory of the new covenant that surpasses the glory of God that was on display in the Law (2 Cor. 3:7–8). The new-covenant era had dawned through Christ, and because of this, the Spirit Himself had been poured out on God's covenant people.

Paul also emphasizes the centrality of Christ in these new-covenant promises (2 Cor. 3:14). Because Christ has taken away the veil that blinded his eyes to the gospel in the Old Testament, Paul says, he was now able to see the glory of the Lord. When he saw this glory, he was transformed (v. 18). Do you see that process? Because God is fulfilling His new-covenant promises in Christ, we are enabled to see Him more clearly, and as we see Him more clearly, we are transformed more fully into the image of Christ.

We can see in Romans that Paul's understanding of the Law is also rooted in the new covenant. In Romans 8:2, he writes, "the Spirit of life has set you free in Christ Jesus from the law of sin and death." Then in verse 4, the "righteous requirement of the law" is fulfilled in us. Some people claim that this "righteous requirement" refers only to the obedience of Jesus that is counted to us. To be clear, the imputed righteousness of Christ is very important. By His obedience to the Law, Jesus did what we could never do. When we are united to Him by faith, His obedience to the Law is counted as our obedience (see, for example, 2 Cor. 5:21). But there is more to our obedience than counting His obedience as our own.

Because we are united to Him and Jesus' obedience is credited to us, we are now able to begin to fulfill the Law ourselves. We see this again in Galatians 6:2, where Paul writes that when we bear each other's burdens, we fulfill the law. This is another way of talking about loving your neighbor as a way to fulfill the "law of Christ." Because Christ has fulfilled the law for us, we can now fulfill the law through Him. That is to say, we can actually reflect the moral principles behind the commands of the Law in our new-covenant obedience.

This new-covenant, Spirit-driven, Christ-focused keeping of the law then becomes the foundation for Christian obedience in Paul's letters. When we read any of his letters, we quickly see that obedience is not optional for a true Christian. He writes that if we continue in unrepentant sin, we will not inherit the kingdom of God (1 Cor. 6:9; Gal. 5:21). Apart from repentance and obedience, we will not be saved.

Paul even calls us "slaves of righteousness" (Rom. 6:18).

Everyone who believes in Jesus has been set free from slavery to sin, but this does not mean we are left to do whatever we want. Because of the new-covenant gift of the Spirit and Jesus' fulfillment of the Law, we are called and enabled to obey. If all this sounds familiar, it should. I hope you're beginning to see how much unity James and Paul really had.

Faithful to the End

Near the end of Romans, Paul expresses a desire to travel to Spain and preach the gospel there (15:24, 28). In the same section, he also asked the Roman church to pray for his upcoming journey to Jerusalem, where he would deliver a gift to the church in Jerusalem as an expression of unity from the primarily Gentile churches he had planted (15:25–33).

We know from Acts that Paul was arrested while delivering this gift in Jerusalem, and he was eventually sent to Rome as a prisoner. It is possible he was executed then, but there is a strong historical tradition that says Paul was released after his first imprisonment in Rome and that he finally made it to Spain. Shortly after this, maybe during his return from Spain, he was arrested again and this time executed in Rome around AD 67.

Even though some scholars argue against its authenticity, most Christians through history (including me) believe that 2 Timothy is Paul's last surviving letter. In it, he makes the famous proclamation, "I have fought the good fight, I have finished the race, I have kept the faith" (2 Tim. 4:7). Like James, Paul remained faithful to his calling until the very end. Like James, his life and death were transformed by the good news of Jesus Christ, and his legacy continues until today.

Chapter 5

THE SHARED MINISTRY OF JAMES AND PAUL

From about 220–200 BC, a mini world war raged across the Mediterranean world. The main powers in conflict were Rome and Carthage, but tribes from modern-day Spain, Greece, Turkey, and North Africa were also involved in what is now known as the Second Punic War. Both ancient and modern historians consider this extended conflict one of the deadliest wars in history, and Rome's eventual victory vaulted them to dominance in the Mediterranean region for centuries to come.

Even though the outnumbered Carthaginians eventually lost the war, early in the war their general Hannibal devised a military strategy that saved them from immediate defeat and that continues to be used today. After surprising the Romans by passing through the Alps and invading Italy from the north, Hannibal's army slowly advanced to the southeast part of the Italian peninsula. In the late summer of 216 BC, a large Roman-led force had gathered at Cannae in Southeast Italy to crush Hannibal's army and end the war.

As the armies faced each other, it was clear that the Romans had far more troops, somewhere over sixty thousand, while the Carthaginians had around thirty-five thousand. A Roman victory was inevitable—or so it seemed. But Hannibal split his army, sending his cavalry away from the main conflict. As the Roman army gradually pressed forward, the Carthaginian general led his forces in a controlled retreat, with the center moving back to gradually form a semicircle around the Romans. Without realizing it, the Roman army had allowed themselves to be surrounded. Once the Roman army was bunched up and unable to move, Hannibal ordered the cavalry to attack the Romans from behind while the main army attacked them from the front and sides.

This "pincer movement," as the tactic is known, brought a resounding victory for Carthage. The ancient historian Livy reported nearly fifty thousand Roman casualties to just eight thousand for Hannibal's army. By using a strategic division of his army, the general was able to win a surprising victory that demoralized the Romans and extended the war for another fifteen years.

When I read about Hannibal's strategic division of his army, I'm reminded of how James and Paul worked together as part of a single army, working toward a common goal while separating the troops for the sake of the greater good. In this chapter, we want to look at all the places in the historical narrative of the New Testament where we find James and Paul together. As we do, we'll see that these two men were remarkably unified in both their mission and message. We might even say they were dividing to conquer.

First Impressions

James almost certainly heard about Paul before his conversion on the road to Damascus. As the new leader of the church in Jerusalem, persecution from Paul had to be one of James's biggest concerns, but after Paul's calling and conversion, they didn't seem to have spent much time together.

We saw earlier that about three years after Paul met Jesus on the road to Damascus, he traveled to Jerusalem to meet with Peter. As we saw, the Christians in Jerusalem did not trust him at first, but Barnabas introduced him to some of the apostles—probably Peter and James—and told them about how Paul was proclaiming the gospel in Damascus (Acts 9:26–27; Gal. 1:18–19).

In Galatians 1:18, Paul tells us that he stayed in Jerusalem for fifteen days, but beyond that, we don't really know much of what Peter and Paul talked about. It is fun to imagine some of the conversations they had over those two weeks. What did Peter tell him about his years with Jesus? What Old Testament passages did they discuss and maybe even debate? Did Paul apologize for his persecution? Did Peter tell Paul about his own betrayal of the Lord? We don't know what all they discussed, but the British New Testament scholar C. H. Dodd was right when he said surely they could not have spent the whole time talking about the weather.[1]

During this early trip to Jerusalem to meet with Peter, Paul did not see any other of the apostles or early Christian leaders except James. Again, we can't know what Paul talked about with James any more than we can know what he discussed with Peter, but it is easy to imagine that they shared stories about their experiences with Jesus, preaching the good news, and what it means to live in the era of God's fulfilled promises.

After a couple of weeks in Jerusalem, Paul left and went to Syria and Cilicia (Gal. 1:21) and ended up back in his hometown of Tarsus before Barnabas brought him back to Antioch (Acts 11:25).

Paul and James didn't see each other again for the next decade or so, but they were both an essential part of the early church and its mission. They had the same coworkers, like Barnabas. They were on the same team and working toward the same goals.

In fact, when Paul was in Jerusalem with Peter and James, they weren't just sitting around talking the whole time. Paul was mingling with the crowds in Jerusalem, "preaching boldly in the name of the Lord" (Acts 9:28). He was so bold in his witness that some of his fellow Jews were trying to kill him.

I have a hard time imagining that Paul's bold witness did not leave an impression with James. Paul says that when the churches in Judea glorified God when they heard about him, it is likely that James was a part of that group. Some biblical scholars paint a picture of early Christianity as a wrestling match between Paul and the Gentiles on one side and James, Peter, and the Jews on the other. The actual witness of the New Testament gives us a very different picture. If Paul and James were in a wrestling match, they weren't opponents; they were tag-team partners, flying together off the top ropes.

Split or Strategy?

The next time Paul and James saw each other was probably about ten years later. At the end of Acts 11, Luke tells us that the prophet Agabus came from Jerusalem to Antioch, announcing a coming famine in Judea. In response to this, the church in Antioch sent Barnabas and Paul to deliver "relief," which was probably food and money, to the church in Judea (Acts 11:29). While they were in Judea, Paul tells us in Galatians 2 he had another meeting with the apostles in Jerusalem (Gal. 2:1–10).[2]

During this private meeting between Paul and the "pillar apostles"—James, Peter, and John—they came to a shared understanding about the gospel and its implications for Gentiles. They all agreed that Titus, who went with Paul and Barnabas to Jerusalem, did not need to be circumcised to be justified. Titus was a Gentile, so they were saying that an uncircumcised Gentile was a member of God's people. For most of us reading Galatians in the modern Western world, this doesn't seem like that big of a deal. But this was a very big deal for first-century Jews.

Jerusalem was becoming a volatile place in the late 40s AD. We see the tension between the Romans and the Jews in the Gospels, and in the decades following that time, things would only get worse. More and more Jews were calling for the overthrow of Roman rule, and this unrest would bubble over into a full-blown revolt in AD 66 that ended with the Romans destroying the Jerusalem temple in AD 70. After other uprisings in the second century, Jerusalem was wiped out.

During this move toward revolution, it was hard to remain neutral. Jews would have been under a lot of pressure to retain their distinct identity as God's people. Circumcision and other markers that separated Jews and Gentiles, while important in the old covenant, took on a new significance during this time and became a form of self-righteousness for many.

In the middle of all this tension, Paul, James, and the other leading apostles all agreed that Titus did not need to be circumcised to be a part of God's people. Paul and James agreed that keeping the whole Law was not a necessary part of Christian obedience. This was revolutionary stuff.

Paul, James, Peter, and John also agreed on a shared strategy for their mission. Paul would go to the Gentiles and James, Peter, and John to the Jews (Gal. 2:9). They all proclaimed the same gospel—we are united by faith alone in Christ for forgiveness of sin and restoration of our relationship with the creator God—and they all agreed that part of their mission was to care for the poor, which is probably a reference to caring for the poor in Jerusalem in particular (2:10). Later in his ministry, Paul would devote a lot of time and attention to this by gathering a collection to care for the poor in Jerusalem.[3] Both James and Paul also

apply the principle of caring for the poor more widely in their
letters.

James and Paul grew up as passionate followers of the God
of Israel, devoted to the purity of the nation, but their lives had
been redirected by the Messiah Jesus. They now recognized that
God's purposes were moving beyond Israel to the Gentile nations. God had called Paul to lead the way in this mission to the
nations, and they both agreed on this when they met privately
in Jerusalem.

Based on the shared strategy that they reached at this meeting, it should not surprise us to see that when Paul and Barnabas
returned to Antioch, they were soon sent out on what we often
call Paul's first missionary journey (Acts 13:1–3). It is right for us
to emphasize that the church in Antioch was the primary sender
and supporter for Paul and Barnabas. We can also see that this
mission was part of the shared missional strategy that Paul and
the apostles in Jerusalem, including James, worked out in their
earlier meeting.

This strategy was reaffirmed later in Acts, after Paul and
Barnabas had returned from their mission. As they traveled
to the island of Cyprus and through the southeastern part of
modern Turkey preaching the gospel, both Jews and Gentiles
were turning to Jesus the Messiah in faith and repentance. Soon,
Paul and Barnabas were not just dealing with individual cases
like Titus. Whole family groups were believing in Jesus and being
baptized; as Luke describes it in Acts 14:27, God "had opened a
door of faith to the Gentiles."

When word about this movement among the Gentiles
reached Jerusalem, some Jewish Christians insisted that to be a
full-fledged member of God's people, you still had to become a
part of Israel.[4] This was just the opposite of what Paul and James
had agreed on earlier. But that agreement was reached in a private

meeting with just a few apostles and their close coworkers; now it was time for the whole church to consider the role of the Gentiles in the end-time people of God.

After the apostles and other church elders gathered together in Acts 15, there was "much debate" (Acts 15:7). As the room began to quiet down, Peter stood up to proclaim how God had given the gift of the Holy Spirit to the Gentiles. Keep in mind that earlier in the book, in Acts 2, Peter saw the outpouring of the Holy Spirit as the sign that God was fulfilling His eschatological promises to Israel (vv. 17–21). Now he was saying that Israel's eschatological gift was also being given to Gentiles without them obeying the Law!

Paul and Barnabas then related their experience on their missionary journey. They may have even described their strategy for reaching the Gentiles. After he heard this report, James again affirmed his agreement with Paul. He saw the inclusion of the Gentiles as the fulfillment of Amos 9:11–12, when the "booth of David that is fallen" was restored in the resurrection, ascension, and reign of Jesus. As a result of this, God was calling "all the Gentiles who are called by my name" (Acts 15:16–17). The Jewish leaders of the early Christian church all agreed: through the risen Messiah Jesus, God was saving the Gentiles, and Paul's mission was a key part of God's redemptive plan.

Several years after this, in his letter to the church in Rome, Paul read in the Old Testament promises in a very similar way to James's conclusion from Amos 9 in Acts 15. Paul wrote that the Messiah Jesus has kept God's promises to Israel's fathers. As a result, the Gentiles glorified God for His mercy (Rom. 15:8–9). Paul goes on to cite a series of promises from the Old Testament that all look to the day when the Gentiles will hope in the restored king who sits on David's throne (2 Sam. 22:50; Deut. 32:43; Ps. 117:1; Isa. 11:10). James and Paul agreed that God is fulfilling His promises to Israel through Jesus with the result that He is also blessing the Gentiles.

James and Paul—and the other apostles for that matter—agreed that when God keeps His new-covenant promises in the reign of Jesus, the true King of Israel, the inclusion of the Gentiles in the people of God results. Not only that, but they are included as covenant members with all the rights and privileges thereunto, without converting to Judaism, without being circumcised, without keeping the Mosaic Law, and so on. Nothing in the New Testament gives us a hint that James and Paul ever disagreed on this question. While Galatians does mention that some "men [who] came from James" were teaching differently (Gal. 2:12), nothing directly attributed to James insinuates that he ever had anything other than total agreement with Paul on this question, and the decision of the Jerusalem Council affirmed this agreement.

After their meeting at the Jerusalem council, we know of only one other meeting between James and Paul. In Acts 21, when Paul traveled to Jerusalem to deliver his collection for the saints, he met with James and the other elders in Jerusalem. Once again, when James heard about all that God had done through Paul's mission among the Gentiles, he and his fellow elders glorified God (Acts 21:20).

James then asked for Paul's help in his mission to the Jews by going to the temple to be purified according to the Law and to demonstrate that as a Jew he was happy to continue keeping the Law. While scholars might disagree about whether Paul himself always kept the ritual parts of the Law, it is clear that his purpose here was missional. He was affirming James's ministry among the Jews and trying to remove a barrier to the gospel from the Jews in Jerusalem. In other words, once again, James and Paul were united in their mission to both Jews and Gentiles. Their "pincer movement" to reach the Roman Empire with the gospel was still in motion.

James and Paul agreed that God was fulfilling Old Testament promises by calling Gentiles to follow Israel's Messiah without becoming citizens of Israel. They also agreed that it was Paul's primary calling to bring the gospel of Jesus to these Gentiles, while James and some of the other leading apostles would continue to focus on the Jews. This does not mean that Paul and James agreed about everything immediately every time they were together. I'm sure that Paul's travels and experiences shaped him in a way that James, who doesn't seem to have ever traveled out of Palestine, did not understand. In spite of this, they remained united in their message and mission.

Rather than splitting over disagreements, everything in the New Testament indicates that they were implementing a shared missional strategy throughout their lives and ministries. Even though this "strategy" was not designed in quite the way Hannibal's strategies for war were, we can see a shared commitment to reach the same goal while pursuing different arenas with the gospel. At the risk of sounding trivial, maybe it was less like a strategy for war, and more like a strategy for putting Legos together.

My third son is the Lego mastermind of the family. Sometimes my wife and I will help him with a robot or spaceship he is building, and he assigns us different colors of pieces to find. Katie might find all the red blocks, and I might gather all the blue ones. We don't really know how it will all come together, but we know that there is a plan that we have a little part in. In the same way, James and Paul picked up pieces from the Jews and Gentiles but trusted God to bring all the pieces together as they proclaimed the same gospel message to both groups. And their agreements go much deeper than this.

As we saw in the previous chapters, both of them taught about the intersecting themes of the new covenant, the Law, and Christian obedience in a remarkably similar way. Both of them clearly taught that Jesus' ministry, death, resurrection, and reign had brought in the age of new-covenant fulfillment. Even though they use somewhat different language to talk about it at times, both James and Paul allude to the new-covenant promises from Jeremiah 31 and other Old Testament prophets. Through Jesus, the new covenant has come, the law has been written on our hearts, and God has given a heart of flesh to replace our heart of stone.

Because the new covenant has been established, both James and Paul see the law in a new light. The law is written on our hearts; therefore, we can keep this new-covenant law. James talks about how we fulfill the "perfect law" (1:25), "the law of liberty" (1:25; 2:12), and the "royal law" (2:8). Paul says that we fulfill the "law of Christ" (Gal. 6:2); because Jesus kept the law, we are now empowered to fulfill its "righteous requirement" (Rom. 8:4). Again, while they use different language, both of these apostles see the new covenant transforming and translating the Law into a law that Christians can and should keep.

For both James and Paul, the fulfillment of the new covenant and the law written on our hearts means that Christian obedience is a necessary part of following Jesus. Both Paul and James affirm that true faith in Jesus is demonstrated by a life marked by faithfulness. This does not mean we are perfect or sinless, because both of them also speak of the need for forgiveness (see, for example, Eph. 4:32 and James 5:15). As we delve more deeply into their writings in part 2, we'll see the new covenant, the Law, and Christian obedience all at work again. For now, we can see Paul and James are singing the same tune on these three inter-related themes.

A Long-Term Strategy

Hannibal's pincer movement in the battle of Cannae defeated the Roman armies. They were initially devastated by this loss but eventually won the Second Punic War because they had the resources to outlast Carthage. When James and Paul employed their "missional pincer movement" to the Jews and Gentiles, it didn't seem like it affected the Roman Empire very much. Both James and Paul were executed by Roman authorities just fifteen or twenty years after the Jerusalem Council. Unlike Hannibal, they did not see the Romans retreating in a panic. This was not the kind of victory they were trying to win. The kingdom that James and Paul were advancing has the resources to outlast Rome and every other empire and nation since. While kingdoms and emperors have come and gone, the gospel has continued to advance because of the foundation that James and Paul laid in the earliest days of the Christian church.

In the chapters that follow, we are going to look in more detail at how James and Paul taught about this great gospel message and its implications. Once again, we will find different emphases in their teaching on justification, but when we put the pieces together, we will find them speaking in a unified voice.

PART 2

The Letters of James and Paul

Chapter 6

ABRAHAM'S FOUNDATIONAL FAITH (GEN. 15:6)

As we've seen, both James and Paul grew up living and breathing the Old Testament Scriptures. They were self-consciously living in the story of Israel, and Israel's story begins with the life of Abraham. The founder or founders of a nation have a powerful place in the ongoing story of that nation, and we like to be able to point to a "founding father" to mark the beginning of our national identity. For many Americans, George Washington's role as the father of United States remains a point of pride. I don't think he has quite the same level of fame, but Lachlan Macquarie is sometimes called the "Father of Australia." In Hawaii, where I used to live and still often minister, King Kamehameha the Great is revered as the king who united the islands and founded the Hawaiian monarchy. Every year on June 11, the state celebrates King Kamehameha Day with a parade and a day off work for many.

Because of this, we should expect Abraham to be prominent in both the Old Testament and other Jewish writings, and this is exactly what we find. Abraham was the "founding father" of Israel. His role was much more than the founding of a nation, because the nation of Israel was not simply one nation among many others. God's covenant with Abraham marked the beginning of His covenant with a particular nation, and He promised to bless the world through that nation. Because of this, God's promises to Abraham are foundational for the rest of the story of the Bible. Time and again, in both Old and New Testaments, the Bible points back to this foundational covenant (see examples in Josh. 1:2–6; 2 Kings 13:23; Ps. 105:5–11; Isa. 49:6; Ezek. 37:21–25; Matt. 22:32; Rom. 11:1; Heb. 11:8–10).

About a century or two before Jesus was born, a group of Jews who lived in Egypt wrote a document called the Psalms of Solomon. These weren't actually written by Solomon the King but used his name to add authority or importance. Psalms of Solomon 9:9 says that God chose "the offspring of Abraham above all the nations, and you placed your name upon us, Lord, and you will not reject us forever."[1] This emphasis on God's covenant with Abraham would have been in the air that James and Paul grew up breathing, and it reflects a hope that we see in many places in the Old Testament. Abraham was not just the founding father of Israel. For James and Paul, not to mention the Old Testament itself, Abraham's life of faith was also the model for followers of the true God. Even if George Washington, Lachlan Macquarie, or Kamehameha the Great don't particularly interest you, this founding father is very important for everyone who is seeking to understand what James and Paul teach about justification and salvation.

Abraham's Call

When we first meet Abraham, he is living near the city of Ur (often called "Ur of the Chaldees"), in the southwestern part of modern Iraq. Like Paul, he had two names: Abram and Abraham.

Unlike Paul, however, God did change his name later in his life. When we first meet him, he is Abram (which means something like "exalted father"). However, in Genesis 17, his named is changed to Abraham ("father of a multitude"). Again, to keep things simple, let's just stick with Abraham.

Many years later, after his descendants had entered the promised land, we learn more about Abraham's early life. In Joshua 24, the Lord announces to the people, "Long ago, your fathers lived beyond the Euphrates, Terah, the father of Abraham and of Nahor; and they served other gods" (v. 2). Though most people in Ancient Mesopotamia worshiped hundreds of gods, the patron god of the city of Ur was the moon (known as Nanna in Sumerian or Su'en in Akkadian). Abraham was born into an idolatrous, moon-worshiping family. The first-century Jewish philosopher Philo says that Abraham was born into a family who thought "the stars and entire heaven and universe to be gods."[2]

In Joshua 24, God continues, "Then I took your father Abraham from beyond the River and led him through all the land of Canaan, and made his offspring many" (v. 3). There was nothing particularly virtuous about Abraham or his family that would win God's favor. Even though they were somewhat wealthy with animals and servants, they did not have any special claim to the throne of Mesopotamia or anywhere else. It appears that Abraham was just another affluent idolater several generations removed from Noah and the flood (see Gen. 11:10–26). However, like James and Paul, Abraham also had a surprising encounter with the living God.

Near the end of Genesis 11, Abraham's father, Terah, moved the family from Ur toward Canaan, from the "Fertile Crescent" west toward the Mediterranean Sea. They first settled about 600 miles northwest of Ur in the city of Haran. Even though this move brought them out of Ur, there is no reason to think that they had abandoned their idolatry after settling in Haran. Abraham had not done anything special to distinguish himself from the nations around him, but God was about to intervene in an amazing way.

Soon after Terah died, the Lord Himself appeared to Abraham and called him to go to what we now call the promised land. For a moon-worshiping farmer from Ur, this was an amazing grace—as it would be for any of us. God told Abraham to leave his family and go to the land God would show him. He promised to make Abraham a great nation, to bless him, and to bless all the families of the earth through him (Gen. 12:1–3). It is important that we don't miss this point. The nations would one day receive the blessing promised to Abraham and his family. God's choice of Abraham and Israel was not ultimately about Abraham and Israel. God chose Abraham and promised to bless him in order to bless the nations, which was a greater part of His plan to restore His fallen creation. The rest of Genesis, and really the rest of the Bible, is the story of God keeping His promise to Abraham for the sake of the whole creation.

Abraham's Faith

When God first appeared to Abraham, he was about seventy-five years old (Gen. 12:4). God had promised to make him a great nation and to fill the land with his offspring. The only problem was he didn't have any offspring. And his wife, Sarah, was only about ten years younger than he was.[3] A seventy-five-year old man and his sixty-five-year old wife were not exactly prime candidates for the parents of the young children's Sunday school class.

Sometime after He had first appeared to Abraham in Genesis 12, God came to him again in a vision to reassure him of His promises (Gen. 15:1). Abraham wasn't quite sure how this could happen, since he still did not have a son, and his servant Eliezer was his heir. God brought Abraham out under the night sky and asked him to count the stars—an impossible task, of course. He assured Abraham that his offspring would be the same way: uncountable (Gen. 15:5). In response to God's promise, Abraham believed. This affirmation of Abraham's faith and God counting him as righteous in Genesis 15:6 became the foundation for both James's and Paul's discussion of justification, so it is important for us to stop and ask what exactly is happening in this chapter.

Whatever else he had thought about God's promises to this point, Abraham's trust in God is evident in Genesis 15. Whether this text is describing what had happened at some earlier point in Genesis 12–14 or what happened in that very moment, the point is the same. Abraham really and truly believed God's promises to him. He really and truly devoted himself to following the Lord and to trusting that what He told him was true. As Brian Vickers describes it, "Abraham's faith is his belief in God, specifically his trust that the one who promised is also able to do what he promised."[4] We'll see in a moment how that belief transformed Abraham's life, but before Abraham took the next step, before he had obeyed God in any other way, God "counted it to him as righteousness" (Gen. 15:6).

The Latin translation of the word "righteousness" here is *iustitia*. If you have seen *Indiana Jones and the Last Crusade*, near the end, Indy has to cross a bridge by walking on the letters to spell God's name "Jehovah." If not, then just go with me here. He almost falls because he forgets that he has to translate the *J* to an *I* (as if a college professor in the 1930s would be that weak in Latin). The point is, when we change the *i* in *iustitia* to a *j* we get *justitia*—justice. This idea of counting or declaring someone to be righteous is where we get the word *justification*. In other words, Genesis 15 describes Abraham's justification, when God declared him righteous.

Remember the place this falls in the story of the Old Testament. God created the world (Gen. 1–2); the world has fallen (Gen. 3); God promises to make the world right again (Gen. 3:15). Through the flood (Gen. 6–9) and the tower of Babel (Gen. 11), God was moving His plan to save His whole creation forward. Then, when God declared Abraham righteous, He was granting Abraham the status of being part of His redeemed creation that will submit to its Creator again. We can and will say more there, but Genesis gives us at least that much.

God counted Abraham as righteous through his faith, and his faith was in God's promise to give him an offspring and to bless the world through that offspring. Rather than declaring him righteous on the basis of what Abraham has done, God recognizes his faith and grants him the status "righteous." The "it" that God counts as righteousness is not simply Abraham's faith, but instead is the *situation* in which Abraham has faith in God's promises. In other words, God doesn't count Abraham's faith as a type of works-righteousness or something like that. He counts Abraham as righteous because Abraham trusts God's promise to bless him and the world. He believes God will do what He says He will do, and God declares him "righteous" as a means of fulfilling those very promises. Abraham was really and truly justified by faith alone.

We don't know exactly how much Abraham understood about how his offspring would bless the world and undo the wrong that sin and death caused (my suspicion is that he understood more than we might think). We do know, however, that Abraham still had a long way to go in his own growth in righteousness. In the next chapter, he agrees to conceive a son with Sarah's servant Hagar. A few chapters later, in Genesis 20, he lies to Abimelech about Sarah being his wife to save his own skin. At the moment when God counted Abraham as righteous, Abraham was far from perfect. God's promises to him were not a wage that he had earned or a reward that he had coming to him. No, God's promises to Abraham were a gracious gift given to an undeserving sinner.

Abraham's Works

Even though we see that he was not perfect and certainly made some big mistakes, this does not mean that Abraham just ticked off the box marked "belief" and carried on with his life as if nothing had happened. In spite of his mistakes, he continued to follow God and—this is really important—he *actually obeyed* God. As we track the rest of his life, we can see that God's declaration that Abraham was righteous started to work itself out in his life, so that Abraham's character slowly changed and started to align with his status before God. Even though he had a son with Hagar in Genesis 16, in Genesis 18, Abraham reiterated his trust that God would give him a son with Sarah, and God kept that promise in Genesis 21. At the end of chapter 18, Abraham intercedes for Lot, his nephew, to save him from God's judgment on Sodom and Gomorrah. But the clearest place where we can see Abraham's obedience flowing from his faith is in his willingness to sacrifice Isaac in Genesis 22.

This story makes many of us, including me, uncomfortable, especially since it's probably the main way that Abraham displays his obedience to God in Genesis. If you aren't familiar with this story, God asks Abraham to take Isaac to the top of a mountain and sacrifice him as a burnt offering. How could God ask him to do this?

We know that God is just to demand the life of each and

every sinner who rebels against Him.[5] And He has the right to test Abraham's commitment to obey Him by asking him to sacrifice Isaac. More than anything, this episode teaches us about how Abraham's trust in God led him to obey God when asked. Later in the Bible, we learn that Abraham expected God to raise Isaac from the dead (Heb. 11:19). At the last second, God stopped Abraham and provided a ram as a sacrifice in place of Isaac (Gen. 22:13).

I know our main point here is to talk about Abraham's faith and obedience, but let's pause to marvel at the picture of redemption that is painted here. God was just to ask for the life of Isaac, a sinner, but He provided a ram to take the place of Isaac. This picture teaches us that God has committed Himself to providing a substitute for the sin of His people. Later, in the Mosaic Law, God instructs His people to offer a bull as a sacrifice on the Day of Atonement as a substitute for their sins (Ex. 29:36). This picture that we see with the ram and the bull is finally fulfilled when Jesus goes to the cross as the substitute for our sins!

Going back to Abraham, his faith in God's promises actually affected the way that he responded to God's instructions. He believed that what God said is true. He believed that God would bless the world through his offspring, and his obedience was rooted in that trust. His righteous status before God led to righteous action in obedience to God. We might even say that God's declaration that he was righteous was later "fulfilled" in his obedient action, when he really did submit to the instructions from God, his Creator and Redeemer. More on this when we get to James's explanation of Abraham. For Abraham, faith and works were inseparable.

Abraham and First-Century Judaism

In the coming chapters, we'll look at how James and Paul read the story of Abraham, but before we get there, it will be helpful to point out one example of how other first-century Jews interpreted Abraham's life. I mentioned earlier that Philo, the Jewish philosopher and (kind-of) theologian, commented on Abraham's previous idolatry. After explaining how Abraham's family was idolatrous and leading him astray, he paints a glowing picture of Abraham as a wise philosopher who reasoned his way to understanding God. Abraham's innate character and tremendous wisdom led him to God. To be fair, Philo does say that Abraham was under the "influence of inspiration," but the picture he paints is beyond what we would call hagiographic. Abraham's own wisdom and virtue led him to be the first person to believe in God, says Philo.[6]

The picture that Philo paints is similar to many other retellings of Abraham's story by contemporaries of James and Paul. They suggest that while he certainly received help and revelation from God, Abraham's calling was largely due to his own merit, virtue, wisdom, or some other positive character quality. In Genesis, however, God's calling and promises come before we hear anything positive about Abraham. These later writers tended to confuse the order of faith and righteousness, and with that came serious misunderstandings of the nature of God's grace. In different ways, both James and Paul were dealing with the problems that sprang from these kinds of misunderstandings.

Abraham's Faith and Works

In Genesis, Abraham really was justified by his faith alone. It is necessary for us to emphasize this truth as we read Genesis. It is also right and necessary to see that the nature of this faith also means that it is impossible to be truly justified without works of obedience that flow from this faith.

We've seen that there is a decisive link between Abraham's faith and God's covenant promises. Abraham believed God's promises, and he was counted righteous before God (Gen. 15:6). We've also seen a decisive link between Abraham's faith and his ongoing loyalty to God. His faith and his righteous status did not exist in a vacuum. His faith was a type of trust that had confidence in God, even to the point of being willing to sacrifice his only son in Genesis 22.

From the perspective of Genesis 12 and 15 looking forward, we can see that Abraham's belief in God's promises was the only necessary condition for him to truly receive those promises and be counted as righteous. Looking back at God's covenant promises from Genesis 22, we also have to say that for Abraham's faith to be authentic, it had to be followed by faithful good works. Not because his works earned God's favor in any way. He already had that. Instead, his works confirmed that his faith was genuine (Gen. 22:12). His works fulfilled God's previous declaration that he was righteous.

With this important background in place, we can turn our attention to James and Paul to ask how they each read Genesis 15:6 and applied it to their readers. As we move forward, it will be important to hold on to both sides of this picture. We will see that James is standing in Genesis 22, looking back at Abraham's faith in God's covenant promises that was confirmed by his ongoing obedience. However, Paul is focused on Abraham's initial belief in Genesis 12 and 15, looking forward to Abraham's works of faith. As we walk through the writings of James and Paul, keeping these complementary perspectives in mind will help us better understand and more faithfully apply James and Paul for ourselves and others around us.

Genesis 15	**FAITH WORKING THROUGH LOVE**	Genesis 22
Abraham believed		Abraham obeyed

Chapter 7

JAMES, JUSTIFICATION, AND FAKE FAITH (JAMES 2:14–26)

For a nine-year-old boy who loved sports and action movies, the summer of 1989 was glorious. Movies like *Batman, Indiana Jones and the Last Crusade, Honey, I Shrunk the Kids, Ghostbusters 2*, and the vastly underrated *Uncle Buck* starring the late, great John Candy all debuted in theaters. That same summer, my family moved into a brand-new house that felt like a mansion to me. And to top it all off, the Detroit Pistons won the NBA championship. For a boy growing up in southeastern Michigan, it couldn't get much better. To this day, I think I can name most of the players on that '89 "Bad Boy" Pistons team. I'm not just talking about the well-known players like Isiah Thomas, Joe Dumars, Dennis Rodman, and Bill Laimbeer, but also the guys on the end of the bench like Fennis Dembo, John Long, and Michael Williams.

Even today, when I think about that team, it brings back great memories. They are often overlooked because they were sandwiched between the Lakers-Celtics rivalry of the '80s and the Michael Jordan Bulls teams of the '90s. They sometimes get a bad rap for their rough play, but that team is one of the greatest of all time. Sure, they were tough defensively and sometimes got a little rough, but they weren't different from many teams of that era. And their offense is vastly underrated. I could go on, and if you ever run into me on the street, I'm happy to make my case further, but a hard truth I need to admit is that my knowledge of the 1989 Detroit Pistons is pretty useless. In fact, this example is probably the most useful thing I can do with it!

I might be able to list ten or twelve basketball players from a team thirty years ago, but I don't know any of those men. I don't have a relationship with them. I can't call them up to talk about the good old days or ask them for NBA tickets. Just knowing about them doesn't help me be a better basketball player. In fact, my knowledge about them is basically useless. I can affirm that Isiah Thomas and Fennis Dembo were NBA champions in 1989, and I would be correct to affirm this. But it doesn't do me any good if I try to step on a basketball court and play like them.

Everything I know about the 1989 Pistons is like the kind of faith that James is arguing against in James 2. It might be true, I might even think it is important, but it is pretty useless.

Doers of the Word

James, the leader of the church in Jerusalem, probably wrote his epistle in the 40s AD to Jewish Christians scattered in the eastern part of the Roman Empire. He was writing to fellow Jews who had come to see that Jesus is the Messiah and fulfillment of the Old Testament. In his letter, James was picking up on and expanding the teachings of Jesus on the kingdom of God present in the church (the promised new-covenant community) through the presence of Jesus (the promised new-covenant Savior) as He sends His Spirit among us.

Near the end of the Sermon on the Mount, Jesus warns that many people will be shocked at the day of judgment when He says to them, "I never knew you; depart from me" (Matt. 7:23). A couple of verses earlier, Jesus explained that the person who enters His kingdom is "the one who does the will of my Father who is in heaven" (Matt. 7:21). If we are going to be recognized as followers of Jesus in the last day, we will do the will of His Father here and now.

If you are concerned that Jesus is teaching works-based righteousness, go back and read the last chapter again. He is not saying anything different from what we saw in our overview of Abraham's faith in Genesis 15. Anyone who is really trusting God will display his or her faith by obedience—doing the will of the Father. James reiterates and applies this same truth in his letter. When James says, "But be doers of the word, and not hearers only" (James 1:22), he is echoing the teaching of Jesus in Matthew 7. And these echoes continue to reverberate into James 2.

Phony Faith

In James 2:14–26, James is responding to some kind of false teaching about the relationship between faith and works. He writes, "Faith by itself, if it does not have works, is dead" (v. 17). He is opposing anyone who claims we can have true faith without good works that follow (vv. 18–20). Some scholars think James is trying to contradict Paul, going so far as to say that when James refers to the "foolish man" in verse 20, he is calling out Paul![1] But we've already seen the substantial agreement that James and Paul have (and we'll see it again). It is probably better to say that he is responding to a misunderstanding of justification by faith alone, regardless of whether his opponents knew anything about Paul.

It is not totally clear who James is arguing with, but we don't have to be able to reconstruct the historical situation of James's audience to be able to understand his main point (which, by the way, is true of the rest of the New Testament as well). In short, James is teaching that fake faith is no faith at all because it is not accompanied by works. It is useless knowledge, no different from knowing the roster of the 1989 Detroit Pistons—and if it is possible, even less useful than that!

James closely connects faith in Jesus, justification, and good works throughout this section. In fact, earlier in chapter 2, James already started emphasizing the necessary works that flow from faith. As we live out our faith in the Lord Jesus, it cannot be marked by partiality (2:1). After giving an example of what it looks like to love our neighbor as a mark of true faith, James turns his argument directly against anyone who might argue that since justification is by faith, good works are not necessary.

James asks, "What good is it, my brothers, if someone says he has faith but does not have works? Can that faith save him?" (v. 14). Notice in the last part of the verse that James is pointing back to a certain kind of faith. "That faith" is a faith that does not produce good works. This "works-less faith" is certainly not the kind of faith we saw in Genesis 15:6, and it is laughable to think that this kind of faith will truly justify anyone. It is phony faith.

As he begins to show how ludicrous this view is, James applies the command to love your neighbor as a mark of true faith in Jesus. If someone has the kind of faith that sees his or her fellow Christians "poorly clothed and lacking in daily food" (v. 15) and sends them away with a smile and a hug but doesn't even try to get them clothes or food, James asks, "What good is that?"

(v. 16). The obvious answer is that it is no good at all. He calls it dead or useless faith.

When I was growing up, my family went on a vacation to Orlando, Florida, home of Disney World and Universal Studios—not to mention many other tourist traps, including Gatorland. At Universal Studios, we took a tram tour around their backlot. Though they weren't filming anything there at the time, we drove past the facade of a house and a city block. As we drove by the front of it, it looked authentic. But when we came around to the back, we saw that it was a fake. It was just a bunch of plywood with flashy paint propped up by some flimsy boards. The faith James is talking about here looks like those buildings. "Go in peace, be warmed and filled" are empty words without a real attempt to care for your brothers and sisters. Just like those backlot facades, that kind of faith is quickly exposed as flimsy and useless.

Justification by What?

In the last part of chapter two, James turns to the Old Testament to demonstrate that for God's people, trust in Him has always resulted in transformed lives. And this leads us back to Genesis 15. Before he gets to Genesis 15:6, James quotes another well-known Old Testament verse, the *Shema* of Deuteronomy 6:4.[2] For centuries both before and after James, even to the present day, faithful Jews would pray, "Hear, O Israel: The Lord our God, the Lord is one." This was Israel's creed, her confession of their one true covenant God.

James was writing to Jewish Christians who would have seen the *Shema* as their fundamental tenet of faith. The argument James was challenging might have been something like, "You want to see my faith on display? I pray the *Shema* every day. And I really mean it!" Well, James answers, even the demons believe that there is one God who made all things. But that knowledge doesn't do them any good. Simply knowing and even believing the truth doesn't accomplish anything. Saving faith is more than this.

Again, we can't know for sure to what or whom James was responding. It is possible that he was answering someone who quoted Genesis 15:6 to prove that all we have to do is "believe" to be justified, but that this belief doesn't need to have any real impact on how we live.

In response to this, James raises the Abraham example. This makes good sense. If Abraham was the model of a faithful believer in the Old Testament, then his example sets the pattern that the rest of God's people should follow. As he reads the Abraham story, it is important for us to see where James is standing in the story. James is picking up the story of Abraham in Genesis 22—many years after Abraham's belief in Genesis 15 (James 2:21). As he applies the example of Abraham, he is looking back from Genesis 22 over the course of several decades to Abraham's belief in Genesis 15.

Abraham was seventy-five when God called him to leave Haran (Gen. 12:4), eighty-six when he tried to take matters into his own hands with the birth of Ishmael (Gen. 16:16), and one hundred when Isaac was born (Gen. 21:5). If we assume Isaac was in his teenage years or older in Genesis 22, as many scholars do, this would be around forty years after God called Abraham.[3] James is asking us to consider what Abraham's faith looked like after forty years of perseverance.

Through the lens of Abraham's mature faith, James asks, "Was not Abraham our father justified by works when he offered up his son Isaac on the altar?" I think statements like this led Martin Luther to say some of the things he did about James. While I understand why Luther was so zealous to protect the doctrine of justification from any hint of works-righteousness, we also have to understand the connections from the story that James is drawing here.

After decades of following God, certainly not perfectly and not without some significant bumps along the way, Abraham's faith was still intact. And God asked him to do what might have seemed impossible. After twenty-five years of waiting for Isaac's birth and after years of raising him, God asked Abraham to sacrifice his son, the one through whom God had promised to bless Abraham, his family, and the whole world. Even in the face of death, Abraham trusted God and did what was asked of him, confident that God's promises would remain, even if he was not quite sure how.

As James reflected on Abraham's faith-fueled obedience, he concludes that this "faith was active along with his works, and faith was completed by his works" (v. 22). Unlike someone who might argue that there is no necessary link between faith and works, James holds faith, works, and justification closely together, because Genesis holds these things closely together. To be sure, he does not collapse them together like some of his fellow first-century Jews who saw Abraham's good works as primary, sometimes even to the exclusion of faith. Even more than this, he does not want us to think that faith and works have nothing to do with each other.

To anyone who might point to Genesis 15:6 in isolation from its context, James is saying, "Do you want to talk about Abraham's faith? Let's think about Abraham's faith forty years after he first believed God's promises." His faith was active, alive, and resulted in obedient action. So then, James can conclude that in Abraham's decades of, to use a familiar but nonetheless true description, "long obedience in the same direction,"[4] his righteous status from Genesis 15:6 was fulfilled or confirmed.

In verse 23, James says that Abraham's obedience in offering Isaac (Gen. 22) was the fulfillment of Genesis 15:6. He is not making any claim that we have not already seen in the context of Genesis itself. Justifying faith is a faith that endures, matures, and acts in loyalty to God. Faith that saves gives us a status that has to be "fulfilled" through good works. In other words, the fulfillment James is pointing to is the realization of Abraham's righteous status by his righteous conduct and character. So then, James cannot be thinking about the initial moment of justification when he talks about faith and works. As we look back over our whole life after that first moment of faith, it will confirm and demonstrate that our initial faith really was and is the kind of faith that saves.

We will return to verse 24 in a moment, but first notice the second Old Testament example that James brings up. Alongside Abraham, the father of the Jewish faith and the paradigm of covenant faithfulness in the Old Testament, we have Rahab, the Gentile prostitute from Joshua 2. Probably not the first person we would choose, is it?

In verse 25, James says that Rahab was justified the same way that Abraham was. By putting a prostitute alongside Abraham, the father of Israel, James beautifully reminds us that any sinner who repents and truly believes is justified. Any repentant sinner is able to demonstrate her faith and righteous status with Spirit-empowered good works. While there may be many reasons why James includes this example with Abraham, Douglas Moo is right to see that these examples teach us "that anyone is capable of acting on his or her faith—whether a patriarch or a prostitute."[5] This is far from a works-based righteousness.

When James asserts that "a person is justified by works" in verse 24, he is looking forward to the same final declaration or "vindication" in the day of judgment that we saw Jesus speaking about in Matthew 7. Again, don't misunderstand. He is not painting a picture where our good works and bad works are put on a giant scale outside the pearly gates so St. Peter can send us to heaven or hell based on which side of the scale tips. Instead, the way that good works serve to justify is by confirming, both during our lives on earth but especially in the last judgment, that we have durable, persevering, good-works-producing faith.

James is not arguing for works-based justification or a justification based on a blend of faith and works. When James says that justification is not by faith alone, he is not denying that faith is the only way that we are granted a righteous status before God. He is denying that the phony faith that he is arguing against here can justify. There is a kind of "faith" that is not really faith. This "faith alone" that does not produce good works is no saving faith at all. It is a useless faith, a fake faith, a dead faith (v. 26).

Genesis 15		Genesis 22
Abraham believed	**FAITH WORKING THROUGH LOVE**	**Abraham obeyed**
Paul		**James**

Back to the Bad Boys

Let's suppose that my knowledge of the 1989 Pistons went beyond knowing their names and numbers. Imagine that I started watching a lot of game film and then went out to the driveway to learn to dribble like Isiah Thomas, shoot like Joe Dumars, or rebound like Dennis Rodman. Over time, my knowledge of them might lead to actual transformation of my basketball skills. Or maybe I could have somehow convinced one of these players to be my personal coach and teach me how to play basketball. That is a knowledge that would be worth something. As my time at the end of the bench on my high school basketball team testifies, none of this ever happened. My knowledge of the 1989 Pistons, sadly, remains a useless knowledge.

This analogy breaks down pretty quickly. Knowing the 1989 Pistons is nothing like knowing one God, the Father Almighty, who made heaven and earth. The point is, just as there is a kind of knowledge that has no real benefit, there is also a kind of faith that is useless. According to James 2, genuine saving faith is a faith that perseveres in its hope in God, just as Abraham did for decades as he waited for God to keep his promises. Real saving faith is a faith that does not remain alone.

Martin Luther never ranked the epistle of James as highly as he ranked Romans, and I'm not sure my argument here would change his mind. He could be a bit stubborn. But I think he would agree with the main application that we're making here. In fact, in his preface to his commentary on Paul's epistle to the Romans, Luther describes true saving faith in much the same way that James does: "Oh, it is a living, busy, active, mighty thing, this faith; and so it is impossible for it not to do good works incessantly. . . . It is impossible to separate works from faith, quite as impossible as to separate heat and light fires."[6]

Just as fire could not be fire without light and heat, so saving faith could not be saving faith without the good works that flow from it. This is the message that we need to hear from James and apply in our churches today and always. And as Luther observes, it is a message that Paul teaches just as clearly.

Chapter 8

PAUL, JUSTIFICATION, AND GODLY GOOD WORKS (GAL. 3 AND ROM. 4)

L ike James and virtually every other Jew in the first century, Paul saw Abraham as foundational to God's entire plan of redemption. They all read Abraham's story in Genesis as a model for how we relate to God and they saw themselves following the pattern established by Abraham. So far, so good. Right?

Yet different people made different points when they read the story of Abraham. As we saw, our friend Philo of Alexandria read Abraham's story as a model of a wise philosopher who, with the help of revelation from God, learned the meaning of true virtue. Rather than teaching us about how to be justified before God, Philo sees Abraham as a shining example of how the Jewish Patriarchs have actually "out-wisdomed" the wisdom of Greco-Roman philosophy. Though he does point to Genesis 15:6, even his explanation of faith seems to fit more with Plato and Aristotle than James and Paul. He concludes that "faith is the queen of all the virtues."[1] In fact, God so admired Abraham for his faith that he responded by trusting Abraham enough to call him his friend. Philo describes faith as a philosophical virtue rather than a trust in God's covenant promises, and to follow his example is to cultivate this virtue, the way Plato followed Socrates. Paul's understanding of Abraham's faith is very different from what Philo describes. We will see in Galatians and Romans that true saving faith means abandoning hope in our own virtue or wisdom and casting ourselves completely and wholly on God's covenant promises.

Galatians

We saw earlier that Paul spent his life traveling to all corners of the Roman Empire, proclaiming the gospel and establishing churches throughout the Mediterranean world. His letters in the New Testament give us a window to how Paul continued to instruct, correct, and encourage these churches and their pastors after moving on to new places. Several of these letters are dealing with urgent problems in the churches, but no letter has as much urgency as his letter to the churches of Galatia, in modern Asia Minor.

At some point after Paul had planted these churches, a group of Jewish Christians had shown up in the region and started teaching that the Gentile Christians would have to keep the Law of Moses in order to be full-fledged members of God's covenant people. This seems to be the opposite of the problem that James was addressing. Paul is dealing with someone who said that we don't enter God's covenant people by faith that is fulfilled through works. Instead, they were saying that both faith and obedience (in this case, obedience to the Law of Moses) is the way we really become a part of (and stay a part of) God's covenant people.

Because he is a faithful reader of the Old Testament, Paul looks at Abraham as an example of how we become a true member of God's covenant people. Unlike James, Paul is not as focused on Abraham's whole life. Instead, he wants to help his readers understand what it means to be declared righteous before God and consequently become a member of His people. And his answer, from Genesis 15:6, is that Abraham was declared to be righteous when he believed God.

Jews, Gentiles, and the People of God

Paul's letter to the Galatians gets right to the point. He reminds them of his calling from God and his status as an apostle who was commissioned directly by the risen Lord Jesus (Gal. 1:1), the same God who called them in the grace of Christ (Gal. 1:6). He is shocked that the Galatians have abandoned the true gospel, because they heard it directly from him, a true apostle (Gal. 1:6). Throughout Galatians 1, Paul reminds them of the miraculous grace of Christ to call him and commission him for his ministry as an apostle. The implication of his calling was that if he was not preaching a true gospel, then the Galatians would not have true faith. They're in this together. If they say that Paul was preaching a false gospel, then their faith was in vain.

Paul's aim in this letter is to remind the Galatians that righteousness before God has always come by faith. He tells them a story that they might have heard already. When Peter was in Antioch, he would eat regularly with Gentile Christians. This would have been a shocking thing to do, especially in the middle of the first century AD in Palestine, where many Jews were especially worried about maintaining their purity from the Gentiles around them.

When Peter ate with Gentiles, he was not just breaking social mores; he was making a profound theological statement, saying that these Gentiles are members of God's people, with no exceptions or qualifiers. Gentiles were declared righteous and included in the people of God without having to keep the Law of Moses. This means that Gentiles were declared to be righteous before God (justified) without having to be circumcised, keep the Sabbath, and abstain from pork, shellfish, and other foods that the Law forbids. This doesn't sound like a big deal to us, but it was a very big deal to them to break these "taboos."

The word *taboo* is linked to the ancient Hawaiian practice of "kapu," which means something like "forbidden things." In ancient Hawaii, women could not eat some foods, like pork, bananas, or coconuts. Or if the shadow of a commoner fell on the house of an ali'i (member of the royal class), then he could be put to death. King Kamehameha the Great made it kapu to cut down certain trees to keep them from being extinct. Maybe the best-known rule of the kapu system is that men and women could not eat together. In fact, their food could not even be cooked together.

Shortly after the death of King Kamehameha in 1819, his son King Liholiho broke the kapu by allowing men and women to eat together. This led to the end of the kapu system altogether, which led to the breakdown of the ancient Hawaiian religious system. I happen to think it was not a coincidence that the first missionaries arrived less than a year later, proclaiming the gospel to the Hawaiians.

Even though God's instructions in the Law were very different from the ancient Hawaiian system, the fear of many of the Jews was probably not that different from the fear of many of Hawaiians who objected to King Liholiho eating with women. If they broke the rules for eating, then the whole system would come crashing down. And you know what? The Hawaiians who thought this were right. Ending the kapus did effectively end the whole

Hawaiian religious system. In a similar way, when Peter was eating with Gentiles, he was also effectively saying that the whole old-covenant system that divided Jews and Gentiles was over.

When "certain men [who] came from James" showed up in Antioch, Peter stopped eating with the Gentiles because he was afraid of the Jews (Gal. 2:12). They were teaching that to really get on God's good side, the Gentile Christians in Galatia had to keep the Law of Moses. Based on what we saw in James's letter, these guys probably weren't really "from James." Instead, they were claiming that to be right with God, we have to keep the Law. They were claiming that justification requires Law-keeping. And then Peter and even Barnabas went along with this. But Paul was not going to stand for it.

When he heard about what Peter had done, he "opposed him to his face" (Gal. 2:11). When Paul saw that Peter and the others were forcing the Gentile Christians to keep the Law in order to eat with their Jewish brothers and sisters and also saw that they were requiring obedience to the Law to be justified. He insisted that this is not consistent with the gospel—in both the Old Testament and New Testament.

When Paul wants to talk about what the Old Testament teaches us about justification, he also turns to the story of Abraham. He reminds the Galatians that they received the Holy Spirit by faith (Gal. 3:2). We saw earlier that the gift of the Holy Spirit was the sign that God is fulfilling His promises to Israel (Acts 2:17–21). Whoever receives the Spirit is a part of God's justified new-covenant people.

The Galatians, like Abraham, were justified and became a part of God's people by faith, not by keeping the Law (Gal. 3:6). Abraham could not have been justified by the Law, because he was declared righteous in God's sight *before* the law was even given to Israel!

While James emphasizes later parts from the story of Abraham to remind us how his status of "justified" was fulfilled by his righteous actions, Paul takes us on a different route. Like James, Paul cites Genesis 15:6 to explain justification, but he starts at a different spot in Abraham's life from James's starting point. Remember, James takes us near the end of Abraham's life, in Genesis 22, when Abraham's obedience was the evidence and fulfillment of his status "righteous."

Instead of jumping ahead in Abraham's life from Genesis 15 to Genesis 22, Paul actually moves back to Genesis 12, where God told Abraham that "in you shall all the nations be blessed" (Gal. 3:8; Gen. 12:3). God had not only declared that Abraham's faith would be the way in which he would be declared right with God (and receive the promised blessing). He also declared that the Gentiles would share in this promised blessing. Let's employ some sanctified logic here: If Abraham received the blessing by faith, then how would the Gentiles receive that same blessing? By faith, of course. Paul is insisting that whether we're talking about Abraham or the Galatians, faith is the only requirement to be justified. In order to be declared to be right before God and therefore a full-fledged member of God's covenant people, we have to trust God's promises. Keeping the Law to *gain* this status confuses the whole picture and ends up adding requirements where God has only said to trust Him.

Genesis 15		Genesis 22
Abraham believed	**FAITH WORKING THROUGH LOVE**	Abraham obeyed
Paul		James

Some biblical scholars argue that when Paul uses the phrase "works of the law," he is talking about keeping the Law in a way that separates Jews from Gentiles so that his main argument is not about legalism but ethnocentric pride. I actually agree with them in a certain way. Paul wasn't debating late medieval Roman Catholicism or some modern version of semi-Pelagianism, which teach that we can change our own hearts. He was debating with some of his fellow Jews who had become Christians, and they disagreed about the role of the Law in the new-covenant people of God. They were saying that keeping the Law is a necessary part of being declared righteous before God—so much so that it was the defining marker of God's new-covenant people.

But, Paul responds, if keeping the Law defines what it means to be the people of God, then there would have been no reason for the Messiah to come and the new covenant to be established. Under the Law covenant, God's people failed to obey God and truly keep His commandments. Because of this, they were under the curse that the old covenant demands for disobedience (exile from the land, the fall of David's monarchy, the departure of God's presence from the people). Paul's argument in most of the rest of Galatians 3 is that if we try to obtain or somehow maintain our justified status before God by keeping the Law, then, like Israel in the Old Testament, we will end up under a curse. The good news for all of us, Jew and Gentile alike, is that Christ became a curse for us (Gal. 3:13). When we have faith like Abraham, we are united to Christ, and His righteousness is counted to us while our sin is counted to Him. He took the curse of the covenant that we all deserve, regardless of our ethnicity. Jesus paid the price for our sin, and as a result, the blessing of Abraham comes to us Gentiles!

When the Galatian Christians were trying to keep the Law to become full members of God's people, they were making at least two mistakes. First, they thought that keeping the Law was a requirement to be right with God. Or maybe a better way to say it is that they thought keeping the Law *could* be a way to be made right with God. But Paul says this was never the case. Abraham was justified by faith apart from keeping the Law. Second, they thought that the Law was meant to be a permanent covenant. Again, Paul explains that the Law was only in place until the Messiah comes (Gal. 3:24). Now that the Messiah has come, if we try to keep the Law, then we are saying that we don't need the Messiah and we can go back to that old covenant to do it our way.

With both of these mistakes, we end up creating a system that puts the burden on us to keep the Law to gain favor with God. Paul is preaching just the opposite. We are made righteous before God by faith, never by our Law-keeping! We might even say that we become a true son or daughter of Abraham by faith, not by keeping the Law (Gal. 3:28).

Romans

Even though Paul's argument in Romans is similar to that in Galatians, his relationship to his audience is different. Instead of trying to convince a church he knows well that they are heading down a path toward destruction, Paul is explaining his overall gospel message to a church he is hoping to meet soon. Although the settings are different, Paul makes many of the same points that he does in Galatians, so we don't need to spend quite as much time in Romans.

In the early chapters of Romans, Paul explains that both Jews and Gentiles need the good news and that both groups are under God's judgment for rejecting Him. His case against the human race culminates in Romans 3:19, where he declared that "every mouth [will be] stopped, and the whole world [will be] held accountable to God." No one is justified by God by keeping the Law (Rom. 3:20). If the Jews try to get or maintain their status before God by keeping the Law, we already saw that would end in death, exile, and curse. Thank God that is not where the story ends.

In Romans 3:21–31, Paul declares that the righteousness of God comes to us through faith. Scholars debate exactly how we should understand God's righteousness here. Some say that it is God's righteous commitment to keep His saving promises to His people. I think the word often has this nuance or implication, but, more fundamentally, the righteousness of God that comes by faith, as Paul puts it in Romans 3:22, is our righteous status before God. Put another way, this verse is talking about justification.

Even though it is not clear in English, the words "righteousness" and "justification" are quite similar in Greek. While I usually tell my students to never use Greek words in their preaching and teaching, I'm going to break my own rule here. In Greek, "righteousness" is *dikaiosune*, and the verb "to justify" is *dikaiao*. We call these "verbal cognates." Okay, Greek class is dismissed.

Whenever Paul is talking about justification, he has righteousness in view. Throughout this section, then, Paul is talking about being declared "righteous" before God, just like he was in Galatians. In Galatians, Paul says that Jesus became a curse for us. In Romans, Paul says that He is our "propitiation," which points back to the sacrifices of the Law (Rom. 3:24–25). Jesus is the ultimate substitute that the animal sacrifices of the Law were anticipating.

Paul's argument is rooted in our union with Christ, which is the foundation of our justification. Jesus is the sacrifice our sin requires. Because of this, God can be both just (because Jesus pays the price sin requires) and the justifier of everyone who trusts Jesus so that they are united to Him (Rom. 3:25). Everything we get in salvation we get because of our union with Jesus. As a result, both Jew and Gentile are in the same boat, and no one can boast (Rom. 3:27).

As he continues to explain God's great gift of justification in Romans 4, Paul turns again to the example of Abraham. If Abraham had kept the Law, had a certain ethnic status, or done anything to earn his status before God, it would not be a gift. Instead, he would be earning a paycheck (Rom. 4:4). Instead, because Abraham believed God, he was counted as righteous (Rom. 4:3; Gen. 15:6). Just as he did in Galatians, Paul insists that Abraham's status before God and his entrance into the covenant people of God was through faith alone.

In Romans 4:5, Paul drives this point home. "And to the one who does not work but believes in him who justifies the ungodly, his faith is counted as righteousness." He does not work. God justifies the ungodly. His faith is counted as righteousness. Paul could not be any clearer. Abraham's status before God had nothing to do with his Law-keeping or obedience, but instead, he was counted righteous because of his faith.

In the second part of Romans 4, he observes that Abraham received circumcision after he had been justified. Abraham's circumcision was "a seal of the righteousness that he had by faith while he was still uncircumcised" (Rom. 4:11). Did you catch that? He had righteousness . . . by faith while uncircumcised. To say he was justified by faith before he was circumcised is another way of saying that he was justified before he kept the Law. Then we can conclude that everyone who believes without being circumcised or keeping the Law gets this same righteous status.

Through his faith, Abraham received the status "righteous," as does everyone else who believes God's promises through the Messiah Jesus, "who was delivered up for our trespasses and raised for our justification" (Rom. 4:25). Abraham is our father, not because he earned his status before God, but because he shows us what it looks like for God to declare us "righteous" apart from our Law-keeping or good works.

Toward the end of the chapter, Paul reiterates this truth once more. Abraham's faith was counted to him as righteousness (Rom. 4:22). The way Paul describes Abraham's growth in faith here sounds very similar to what James describes. Romans 4:20 tells us that Abraham "grew strong" in his faith. His faith and maturity grew, and he did not doubt God's promise, even when he had every reason to do so. He was about one hundred years old and Sarah was ninety. Yet he was "fully convinced that God was able to do what he had promised" (Rom. 4:21). Then look closely at the next verse: "That is why his faith was 'counted to him as righteousness.'" What is "that"? It is a maturing faith, a faith that is fully and increasingly convinced of God's promises. Paul saw a growth in Abraham's faith from the moment of his belief to the birth of Isaac and beyond. His continued growth and maturity demonstrated that his faith was authentic. He was counted righteous because he had true faith, the kind of faith that grows and is demonstrated by good works.

Apart from Galatians and Romans, Paul doesn't quote Genesis 15:6 anywhere else in his letters, but he does bring up justification several other times. The best known justification passage outside of Romans and Galatians is probably 2 Corinthians 5:21. As he concludes a reflection on his calling and ministry, Paul grounds everything he accomplishes in ministry in the new creation, which is accomplished through Christ's work of reconciliation on the cross, where "he made him to be sin who knew no sin, so that in him we might become the righteousness of God." When we are united to him, Christ takes our sin, and we receive the very righteousness of God. He took the status "sinner" to pay for our sins, and we are given the status "righteous" because we are joined to Him by faith. This is what the early Christian letter of Mathetes to Diognetus calls "the sweet exchange."[2]

What about Christian Obedience?

We see that both Paul and James agree that being declared right before God requires trust in His promises. James adds that this declaration is going to work itself out by our good works. Our justified status is fulfilled by our good works. Paul insists that our status before God does not depend on our Law-keeping but is only through our faith. What gives? Have we finally found the dreaded contradiction between James and Paul?

Well, sorry to disappoint, but we need to keep reading Galatians and Romans. As we saw earlier, Paul has no room for a faith that does not produce good works. In Galatians 5–6, Paul again uses language that is remarkably similar to what we see in James 2. In Galatians 5, Paul talks about the "hope of righteousness" (v. 5). If we have righteousness in our initial moment of justification, then why should we still hope for righteousness? Like James, Paul is implying that our justification is fulfilled in our ongoing faithfulness. So there seems to be a future aspect to our justification—call it the final declaration, when our works will demonstrate our true faith and righteous status.

Later in the chapter, he writes that we ought to serve one another in love, "for the whole law is fulfilled in one word: 'You shall love your neighbor as yourself'" (Gal. 5:14, quoting Lev. 19:18). Even though he spent much of the letter explaining that we are justified by faith, not by works of the Law, he now commands the Galatians to fulfill the law! Later, while instructing the Galatians how to care for each other, he tells them that by bearing one another's burdens they will "fulfill the law of Christ" (Gal. 6:2).

We find similar patterns in Romans. Even in Romans 4, Abraham "grew strong in his faith," which points toward some sort of growth (Rom. 4:20). Even though he had the status "righteous," Abraham was still growing. Paul goes on to say that the reason his faith was counted to him as righteousness is that Abraham was "fully convinced" that God would keep His promise, and he continued to grow in faith (vv. 21–22). We might even say that Abraham's righteous status was "fulfilled" by his continued growth in faith.

Even though we are justified by faith, later in Romans, Paul still expects that we ought to "fulfill the law." In Romans 8:3, he says that Jesus has done what we could never do. As a result, he tells us in verse 4, the righteous requirement of the law is fulfilled in us as we begin to obey God from the heart. He clarifies what this means later in the book, when he again points to the command to love our neighbor as the fulfillment of the law, again concluding that "love is the fulfilling of the law" (Rom. 13:10). In both Romans and Galatians, Paul insists that if we have true faith, we will, in some way, fulfill the law—that is, we will actually do what God commands.

The Sweet Exchange

In the coming chapters, we will take some of the exegetical pieces we've seen in the last three chapters and pull them together. Before we move forward, we should not move too quickly past the glory of what we have seen here. God justifies sinners. Through Jesus the Messiah, He grants us, Jews and Gentiles alike, who are unable to keep His Law, the status of righteous and therefore makes us part of His covenant people. By the power of His Spirit, we are enabled to live out this status as we are transformed into the image of Jesus.

This great Trinitarian work of justification is truly glorious. I alluded to a passage from the early Christian *Epistle to Diognetes* earlier, but it is worth returning to that as we wrap up this section:

> When our unrighteousness was fulfilled, and it had been made perfectly clear that its wages—punishment and death—were to be expected, then the season arrived during which God had decided to reveal at last his goodness and power (oh, the surpassing kindness and love of God!). He did not hate us, or reject us, or bear a grudge against us; instead he was patient and forbearing; in his mercy he took upon himself our sins; he himself gave up his own Son as a ransom for us, the holy one for the lawless, the guiltless for the guilty, the just for the unjust, the incorruptible for the corruptible, the immortal for the mortal.
>
> For what else but his righteousness could have covered our sins?
>
> In whom was it possible for us, the lawless and ungodly, to be justified, except in the Son of God alone?
>
> O the sweet exchange, O the incomprehensible work of God, O the unexpected blessings, that the sinfulness of many should be hidden in one righteous person, while the righteousness of one should justify many sinners![3]

PART 3

The Legacy
of James and Paul

Chapter 9

FAITH, WORKS, AND JUSTIFICATION

In the 1990s, Rich Mullins's music stood out among many other Christian musical artists, not only because of his unique, kind-of-folky sound, but also because of the depth and substance of his lyrics. He had a way of making well-known theological truths and their implications come alive for me during my high-school years. But he introduced some new concepts to me as well. For example, I grew up as a low-church Baptist, and to be honest, listening to his *Songs* album around in the late '90s is probably the first time I remember hearing about the Apostles' Creed (to be fair, I may have missed it somewhere along the way). To this day, when I say the Creed with my family in morning or evening prayer, it is at least partially because of Rich Mullins's song "Creed." Another song on that same album was called "Screen Door." This one left me a little uncomfortable. Even though I think I liked it, I didn't quite know how to evaluate the way he sang about faith and works. As I look back on it now, I think I understand and like that song more than I did when I was in high school. Find it and listen to it. He says that faith without works is like "a screen door on a submarine."[1] It's worthless. As I hope you've already seen in this study, it not only captures James's teaching on justification, but it also reflects the letters of Paul well.

Now that we've let James and Paul speak for themselves, it's time to bring them together. Though I won't be as poetic or clear as Rich Mullins, in this chapter I will summarize what we've seen so far, especially in our last few chapters on faith, works, and justification. After we summarize what we've seen in the epistle of James and the letters of Paul, we'll then be able to map out the way that theologians have talked about the doctrine of justification to understand how James and Paul fit into this discussion. Finally, we'll be able to answer the pressing question my seventeen-year-old self was asking: is "Screen Door" really a good song?

James and Paul

James writes that a kind of empty intellectual assent that does not result in good works is a faith that can never justify: "If you really fulfill the royal law according to the Scripture, 'You shall love your neighbor as yourself,' you are doing well" (James 2:8). This royal law is nothing short of the new-covenant reality of God's law written on our hearts by the Holy Spirit (James 1:21, 25). James also emphasizes caring for the poor and vulnerable as the evidence of God's grace in our lives: "Listen, my beloved brothers, has not God chosen those who are poor in the world to be rich in faith and heirs of the kingdom, which he has promised to those who love him? But you have dishonored the poor man. Are not the rich the ones who oppress you, and the ones who drag you into court?" (James 2:5–6). If we are not caring for the poor, the widows, and the orphans—the people around us who cannot sustain themselves—then we are demonstrating that our faith is phony. And James was arguing against just this kind of phony faith.

We could say that James was combating a false faith that fails to give works their proper place as the necessary fruit of saving faith. Rather than seeing how faithful works are the inevitable fruit of faith, James's opponents apparently said that the only thing God requires for justification is that we affirm the facts of the gospel. Maybe they even cited Abraham's faith in Genesis 15 as proof.

When James reads the story of Abraham, he does not skip past Abraham's faith in God's promises or ignore the status that God granted Abraham through his faith. Abraham really did believe that God's promises were true, and God really did count Abraham as righteous and therefore a part of His covenant people (Gen. 15:6). The moment he believed God's promises, Abraham's status before God was "righteous." But this righteous status had to be "fulfilled." If Abraham claimed to believe God but failed to obey Him, then he would have proven that his faith was fake and that his justification was a sham.

We must be careful not to say that James thought Abraham's obedience somehow *earned* his status before God; that was already granted by faith on the basis of God's promises. Instead, Abraham's obedience *confirmed* or *fulfilled* the status God had already graciously given to him. He was actually beginning to evidence his status as righteous through his good works. When this righteous status was fulfilled in his obedience, it proved that Abraham's faith was a real saving faith. Even though Abraham's righteous status was given by faith, this faith could never remain alone. Works need to show for the faith.

While James is arguing against phony faith, Paul is arguing against phony works that are rooted in a failure to see that faith is enough. Paul's opponents did not understand that justification is by faith alone. Instead, they thought good works mixed with faith were somehow part of what God requires in order to declare His people righteous.

Paul's ministry and writings came in a different context and addressed different concerns than James's, but we also saw a lot of continuity with James. Paul certainly teaches that justification is by faith alone apart from works of the Law (Rom. 3:28; Gal. 2:16). He also insists that genuine, justifying faith is "seal[ed]" (Rom. 4:11). It is marked by ongoing hope (Rom. 4:12). Pauline faith must work through love (Gal. 5:6). In fact, Paul sees loving one another as the primary way new-covenant believers who have received the Holy Spirit fulfill the law (Rom. 8:4–5; 13:9). Like James, Paul emphasizes that caring for the poor, widows, orphans, and the vulnerable is an essential fruit of saving faith (Rom. 15:26; Gal. 2:10). Remember, Paul and the apostles in Jerusalem agreed that caring for the poor was a priority in their ministry, so both James and Paul emphasize this as an important area of good works that flow from faith.

Paul, like James, was reading Genesis 15:6 faithfully. Abraham was declared righteous through his faith. However, when Paul applies this truth in Romans and especially in Galatians, he is coming from a different angle. Instead of asking whether we can have saving faith without faith-fueled good works, Paul is asking whether our faith is the only way that we are united to Jesus and declared righteous before God. To this question, he gives a resounding yes. We are declared righteous before God through faith, not works.

However, when Paul reads the story of Abraham, he does not ignore Abraham's ongoing faithfulness. In the last part of Romans 4, we saw that Abraham's faith was growing to full conviction, and this was on display especially when God asked him to sacrifice Isaac. Paul's reading of Abraham's growth in faith is actually very close to James 2. Romans 4:20 tells us that Paul "grew strong" in his faith. James 2:17 and 26 tells us that faith without works is dead. Both are emphasizing that the kind of faith that truly justifies is a faith that requires ongoing growth. Both James and Paul would say that true justifying faith can never remain alone.

Minimizing Sin

James was opposing the false teaching that minimized the need for works that flow from faith, and Paul was opposing the false teaching that requires both faith and works as a necessary part of our initial justification. But both of these false teachings are more similar than we might realize at first. Both perspectives minimize the seriousness and power of sin.

James's opponents minimized the seriousness and power of sin by assuming that a transformed life does not matter after we believe the gospel. As long as we say the right things and maybe even feel the right feels (depending on whatever your particular tradition emphasizes), then we don't have anything to worry about. Sin is really not that big of a deal. James would condemn that way of thinking to hell. If we are not transformed by our faith and if our righteous status is not fulfilled by our ongoing growth in holiness, then our so-called faith is literally demonic.

Paul's opponents also minimized the seriousness and power of sin, but in the opposite way. They did not assume a transformed life doesn't matter; they assumed that it was the only thing that matters—or at least they assumed that it was necessary before God will truly accept us. They taught that sinful men and women can somehow do enough to earn their righteous status by keeping the Law and/or protecting the uniqueness of their ethnic status. If our actions or ethnicity are an essential part of gaining a righteous status before God, then sin is really not that big of a deal. If we can overcome it ourselves to gain God's favor, then the credit ultimately goes to us. Paul also condemns that way of thinking. In Galatians, he calls this another gospel. And anyone who teaches another gospel is accursed, condemned, or, to be frank, damned to hell (Gal. 1:9).

The solution to these problems is not to run away from good works because of the temptation of legalism or to try to do more to win God's favor. Instead, the solution to both is to see the gospel and its implications more clearly. A clear understanding of the all-sufficient work of Jesus as the perfect and necessary sacrifice for sin crushes our failure to take ongoing sin seriously (James's opponents) and the assumption that human good works or status can somehow gain God's favor (Paul's opponents). Both James and Paul see the gospel, which demands that we respond with the kind of faith that produces good works, as the solution to these problems. And both men agree that the life-transforming power of the gospel is on display clearly in Abraham's justification and subsequent growth in faith and obedience, just as it will be on display in everyone else who truly believes.

Faith, Works, and Justification

Till this point, I've avoided summarizing the doctrine of justification or using many abstract theological terms with the hope that we could let the biblical texts speak for themselves. You can decide how successful we've been with that. At some point, however, we have to pull the pieces together.

James and Paul were dealing with different challenges to faith, works, and justification. James was explaining the difference between phony faith—faith that only gives lip service—and real, saving faith. When Paul talks about faith, he always refers to true saving faith. While James contrasts genuine faith and fake faith, Paul does the same with works. What he calls "works of the law" are what we can call phony works. They are works that try to win favor with God and gain us a place in His covenant people. The problem is these don't actually do us any good. When James talks about works, he always refers to works that flow from faith and fulfill our righteous status.

So then, when James and Paul talk about justification, they

are looking at different points in a believer's life, using Abraham as the model. For James, justification is God's declaration that we are declared righteous. Our righteous status is given through faith (Gen. 15:6). However, James also insists that if this status is authentic, it will be "fulfilled" by our works. He emphasizes our good works that flow from true saving faith.

Paul agrees, but he tends to emphasize God's initial declaration when we first believe. However, he does not hesitate to teach that our righteous status will be demonstrated or proved through our faithful good works, which then declare our status on the day of judgment.

	FAITH	WORKS	JUSTIFICATION
JAMES	Exposing phony faith that cannot justify	Emphasizes works that flow from faith	God's initial declaration fulfilled through a life of faithfulness
PAUL	Emphasizes faith in Christ alone as the means of justification	Exposes phony works that cannot justify	God's initial declaration, which will be demonstrated in life and confirmed at final judgment

Defining Terms

Now we can finally move toward defining the doctrine of justification. According to both James and Paul, in our initial moment of justification, we receive the status "righteous" through faith. Both James and Paul agree that justification is a declaration of our status. It is what theologians call a "forensic declaration."

When we hear the word *forensic*, we might think of when a

detective on a TV crime drama will call in the forensics team. We might think of the forensics team or the forensic report in the context of investigating crime. But the goal of these investigations is to gather evidence to present in court. The word *forensic* itself refers to a law court. When we use it in theological context, we are referring to God's eschatological court of judgment. Justification is God's declaration in His "courtroom" that we have the status "righteous."

The moment Abraham believed God's great promises pointing toward the Messiah Jesus, he was declared righteous, his sins were forgiven, he was right with God, and he was a part of God's covenant people. Justification, then, is God's declaration first that we are righteous in His sight and then by implication that we are a part of His covenant people. However, James also says that justification requires faith and works, and Paul talks about a hope for a future righteousness (Gal. 5:5). Justification, like so many other doctrines in the New Testament, is both "already" and "not yet."[2] That is, God's new-covenant promises have *already* begun to be fulfilled through Jesus, but they are *not yet* complete. Many people illustrate this concept by talking about the time between the Allied invasion of France on D-Day, June 6, 1944, and Nazi Germany's surrender on May 8, 1945. The war was essentially over, but there was still almost a year of combat left. Or think of the end of the American Civil War. Robert E. Lee's army of Northern Virginia surrendered on April 9, 1865. The Civil War was over, right? Not so fast. Other Confederate armies continued to fight until November, when the last Confederate soldiers surrendered. Many soldiers on both sides died after Lee surrendered. The point is, in the gap between the already and the not yet, a lot can happen.

We are declared righteous before God through our faith. This faith is our trust that God keeps His covenant promises through Jesus' life, death, resurrection, ascension, and reign as King. In His work to redeem us, He took our sin on Himself. We could say that sin was "counted" to Him. We then receive His righteous status because we are united to Him, the only truly righteous one. This is what many call "double imputation." Our sin is imputed to Jesus, and His righteous status is imputed to us. He gets what we have coming to us (judgment), and we get what He has coming to Him (blessing and life).

Theologians argue about the best way to talk about this, but I'm still convinced that the doctrine of imputation that was clarified in the Reformation is the most helpful way to summarize what Paul in particular is teaching.[3] We are united to Christ by faith, so we receive the status that He has won: righteous before God. The implication of our union with Christ is that His righteous status is counted as our own. This imputation is the "already" of our justification.

However, there is still more to come. Our righteous status, to use James's language, needs to be fulfilled. To be clear, this does not mean that our "justification" (status as righteous) and "sanctification" (growth in righteousness) are two ways of saying precisely the same thing. Instead, we could say that our righteous status requires a transformed life. If we are truly declared righteous through faith in Jesus, then we are truly united to Him. In Romans 6, Paul says that our baptism symbolizes and seals this union. Just as Jesus died and rose again, our baptism is a death and resurrection into Christ so that we have a mysterious but real union with Him. I'm tempted to use an illustration of two people who are handcuffed together in a movie, but don't want to wander into heresy. Let's just say that because we are really united to Jesus, we go where He goes and we get what He gets.

When we are united to Christ, we receive the same verdict before God that He did. He is the Righteous One, and we share

His righteous status. Our union with Jesus also demands that we will be transformed into His image. We might even say that justification and sanctification are two distinct but inevitable outcomes of our union with Christ.

In his magnum opus, *The Institutes of the Christian Religion*, John Calvin helped me better understand the relationship between justification and sanctification. Calvin writes,

> Although we may distinguish them, Christ contains both of them inseparably in himself. Do you wish, then, to attain righteousness in Christ? You must first possess Christ; but you cannot possess him without being made partaker in his sanctification, because he cannot be divided into pieces (1 Cor. 1:13). Since, therefore, it is solely by expending himself that the Lord gives us these benefits to enjoy, he bestows both of them at the same time, the one never without the other. Thus it is clear how true it is that we are justified not without works yet not through works, since in our sharing in Christ, which justifies us, sanctification is just as much included as righteousness.[4]

For centuries, Protestants and Roman Catholics have debated the exact nature of our justification. Roman Catholics have argued that the righteousness given to Abraham was "infused." If I am drinking lemon-infused water, then it is water that has lemon mixed into it. I'm not exactly sure what the difference is between lemon-infused water and lemonade. Anyway, Roman Catholics might say that righteousness is actually "mixed into" us. That is, justification is an actual transformation of our nature or character.

Reformed Protestants have emphasized that this righteousness was declared or imputed to Abraham on the basis of Christ's own righteousness. Theologians call this "alien righteousness."

Not an alien like E.T., but alien in the sense of something that comes from somewhere else. Justifying righteousness is a righteousness that comes from outside of us first; only after we are declared righteous through Christ is our character transformed.

You can probably guess which side of this debate I land on. While moral transformation is necessary, if we are not making the distinction that the New Testament makes between justification and transformation (or sanctification), we are in danger of falling victim to the same errors that Paul was debating.

Without a doubt, there are many differences between first-century Jewish Christians who claimed their Law-keeping and ethnicity combined with faith were the foundation for justification and sixteenth-century Roman Catholics, who claimed their good works combined with faith were the foundation for their justification. However, their fundamental error is still similar, because both saw faith plus something else as necessary to be justified. Both James and Paul would wholeheartedly disagree with both of these views.

These apostles would also wholeheartedly—and maybe even more strongly—disagree with anyone who says that we can be ultimately saved apart from faith-fueled good works. Again, I want to be careful and clear here: justification is by faith alone. We are declared righteous through our trust in God's promises in Christ *alone*. But this declaration of our righteous status must not remain alone. It will produce good works. Whether we live for just a few moments, like the thief on the cross who rebuked the other criminal for mocking Jesus, or for decades, like Abraham who grew strong in faith and fulfilled his righteous status with faithful works, our faith will bear fruit. As John Piper rightly concludes, "Let us make no mistake: Our works of love are *necessary*."[5] We will not be saved apart from our works of love.

Describing Justification

At this point, we still have not defined justification. We are
getting there. It seems to fit the spirit of this book well if we
pull together two different definitions. First, J. I. Packer defines
justification as "a judicial act of God pardoning sinners (wicked
and ungodly persons, Rom. 4:5; 3:9–24), accepting them as just,
and so putting permanently right their previously estranged relationship with himself. This justifying sentence is God's gift of
righteousness (Rom. 5:15–17), his bestowal of a status of acceptance for Jesus' sake (2 Cor. 5:21)."[6] To complement this, Michael
Bird provides a helpful five-fold description of justification that
coincides with what we have observed:

1. Justification is *forensic* as it denotes one's status, not
   one's moral state.
2. Justification is *eschatological* in that the verdict of the
   final judgment has been declared in the present . . . .
3. Justification is *covenantal* since it confirms the promises
   of the Abrahamic covenant and legitimates the identity
   of Jews, Greeks, Barbarians (and even Americans!) as
   full and equal members of God's people.
4. Justification is *effective* insofar as moral sanctification
   cannot be subsumed under justification but neither can
   they be absolutely separated. . . .
5. Justification is *trinitarian* because it is "God who justifies" (Rom 8:33).[7]

If I can attempt to reword these two less-than-concise definitions into an even-less-concise definition—maybe we should
call it a description—we can say: *Justification is the triune God's
forensic declaration that we are righteous; this declaration has
been brought from the day of judgment into the present and*

therefore makes us part of God's covenant people right now. This then guarantees that our righteous status will be confirmed by our growth in love and faithful good works.

Screen Door

Many, many, many books—maybe too many—have been written about Paul's doctrine of justification, but these usually do not give much attention to James. Many books have also been written about James on justification. Even though these usually interact with Paul, they don't always demonstrate the deep unity Paul and James share. We've seen that James was not reacting to Paul's teaching, as some scholars argue, and that Paul was not a radical who rejected James's teaching on the necessity of works. They were both reading Genesis faithfully and both applying it in their own contexts with pastoral wisdom.

Both James and Paul see that in Genesis 15:6, Abraham was truly declared righteous through his faith. He had been forgiven and had been granted a righteous status before God. Both James and Paul recognize that Abraham's faith was pointing forward to the promised Messiah Jesus. Everyone who trusts in God's promises in Jesus, like Abraham, truly receive a righteous status through faith. Finally, both James and Paul teach that this status will be progressively fulfilled in the ongoing life of faithful good works for every believer.

Rich Mullins's "Screen Door" used to make me a little nervous. I thought maybe it sounds too Roman Catholic, and we shouldn't say that faith is one hand and works are the other. In any case, the point of the song is exactly the point of what we've seen in both James and Paul: faith without works is useless.

Chapter 10

PREACHING AND TEACHING JAMES AND PAUL THROUGH THE CENTURIES

In the centuries following James's and Paul's lives, ministries, and writings, the earliest Christians consistently read and taught from both James and Paul. Some heretical groups might have minimized Paul's influence or rejected some of his letters, but almost all Christians everywhere have accepted his writings as authoritative Scripture. In the New Testament itself, Peter calls Paul's writings "Scripture." When he was talking about Paul's letters, Peter says, "There are some things in them that are hard to understand, which the ignorant and unstable twist to their own destruction, as they do the other Scriptures" (2 Peter 3:16). Even though James's letter was not universally recognized as quickly as Paul's writings, all early Christians recognized his authority as an elder in the Jerusalem church, and it did not take long for the whole church to recognize that his letter was Scripture as well.[1]

The earliest Christian writings after the New Testament—typically called the "Apostolic Fathers"—refer often to Paul's letters, but they do not mention James nearly as much. This should not be surprising. After all, there are more *verses* in Paul's letters (2,044) than there are *words* in James (1,742). We have more than fifteen times as many words from Paul as from James.[2] We should expect the earliest church fathers to refer to Paul's letters far more often.

More importantly, the early church accepted James's letter as authoritative Scripture almost immediately. By AD 367, Athanasius—a leading theologian and leader in the church—had no doubts about its place in the canon. Along with Paul's letters, it was included in the list of New Testament books that the whole church accepted as Scripture, and James and Paul have been valuable for teaching and encouragement in the church in the centuries since. We simply don't have any evidence that the church ever rejected James from the list of New Testament books. But this doesn't mean no one noticed the possible tension between James and Paul before Martin Luther.

Teaching James and Paul

Christian theologians have always insisted that if we are going to teach the letters of James and Paul faithfully, we must explain how their teachings about faith and works fit together. In about AD 350, Cyril, bishop of Jerusalem, emphasized that Abraham's faith and works were inseparable: "Abraham was justified not by works but by faith. For although he had done many good things, he was not called a friend of God until he believed, and every one of his deeds was perfected by faith."[3] Like us, he was reading James and Paul together.

Just a few decades later, near AD 400, the great theologian St. Augustine of Hippo wrote a commentary on James, which has been lost to us, unfortunately. Many of his writings on Paul have survived, and even in those he saw the importance of teaching both James and Paul in his church. In his work *On the Christian Life*, Augustine emphasizes the need to preach from both James and Paul. "Holy Scripture should be interpreted in a way which is in complete agreement with those who understood it and not in a way which seems to be inconsistent to those who are least familiar with it. Paul said that a man is justified through faith without the works of the law, but not without those works of which James speaks."[4] When teaching on Romans, he adds that justification by faith without works "must not be understood in such a way as to say that a man who has received faith and continues to live is righteous, even though he leads a wicked life."[5] Augustine thought it is the duty of the Christian preacher to demonstrate how James and Paul have a unified message on faith and works.

St. Bede, often called the "Venerable Bede," wrote a commentary on James in the early AD 700s. In it, he argues that James was actually explaining Paul's teaching. Both James and Paul wanted "to show that the patriarch [Abraham] also performed good works in the light of his faith."[6] In other words, just as we have observed, Bede taught that James and Paul have a unified message in their teaching on faith and works.

Sometime around AD 900–1000, a lesser-known teacher named Andreas the Presbyter either wrote or compiled a series of comments on James. Just as we have throughout this book, Andreas observed that the key difference between James's and Paul's application of Genesis 15:6 was the *timing* of Abraham's faith and works. He calls justifying faith "prebaptismal faith" and insists that faith and works are a necessary part of "postbaptismal faith."[7]

All of these great teachers of the church insisted that both James and Paul need to be heard clearly and that when they are heard clearly, they fit well together. From Cyril to Augustine to Bede and Andreas, the testimony of the first millennia of church history is that both James and Paul teach that Abraham was truly saved by his faith alone but that his faith did not remain alone. After someone believes (and is baptized, the visible sign that accompanies belief, according to Andreas), this faith would inevitably produce good works.

To be clear, I don't want to imply that the early church fathers had a statement on justification that sounds just like the Westminster Confession of Faith. They were dealing with different questions, gave different answers, and sometimes understood justification by faith differently from how I have presented it in this book.[8]

Even though they may have had different understandings about the precise meaning of faith, works, and justification, the consistent teaching of the church during its first millennia was that salvation is by faith, not works, yet it always results in good works.[9] In his recent book on justification, Michael Horton points out that many early church fathers referred to the "sweet exchange" from the *Epistle to Diognetus* that I quoted earlier, and in so doing, emphasized that salvation is through faith alone, not by works.

While this is not the time and place to walk through the history of the Reformation, the great accomplishment of the Protestant Reformers was to recapture and clarify the doctrine of justification by faith alone that had been confused and, in some places, completely lost during the late Medieval period.

Michael Horton points out that Thomas Aquinas, the great doctor of the Roman Catholic Church, concluded in his comments on 1 Timothy 1:8 that Paul is teaching that justification is by faith alone.[10] However, while Thomas and others continued to use the language of faith alone, in their understanding, faith sometimes included works of love that complete faith. This blurring of the lines eventually led to the distortions that the Protestant Reformers needed to address. Rather than bringing more clarity about the nature of justifying faith that results in good works, the Church increasingly confused the relationship between faith and works. By the time Martin Luther entered the priesthood in the early 1500s, many Christian theologians had a poor understanding of the nature of faith and works. The great contribution of the Reformation is that men like Luther, Calvin, Zwingli, and others clarified that the Bible consistently teaches that justification is by faith alone apart from any works.

Although some Roman Catholics were willing to dialogue with Protestants and try to reach a shared understanding of justification, when the Roman Church finally produced their official response to the Protestant Reformation after the Council of Trent, they (somewhat ironically) went back on centuries of tradition and outright denied that Scripture (and the Church) taught that God saves us by faith alone apart from works. Instead, the Council decreed, "man through Jesus Christ, in whom he is ingrafted, receives in that justification, together with the remission of sins, all these *infused* at the same time, namely, faith, hope, and charity."[11]

In reaction to the Reformers, the Roman Church lost its true catholicity, for they no longer affirmed the universal position that faith and works are distinct. They failed to see that justification or salvation is first a status granted by God through faith. Instead, they insisted that faith, hope, and love are "infused at once." Rather than affirming the New Testament's teaching that justification is a status granted through faith in the work of Jesus and fulfilled through faith-fueled good works, they claimed that good works are a necessary condition to reach that status.

I know it can seem like a fine line, but when we say that the addition of hope and love are necessary *before someone is truly justified* and therefore before they are really counted righteous before God and truly a member of God's covenant people, then we are undermining the doctrine of justification by faith alone. This is why the Reformers reacted so strongly.

Admittedly, these strong reactions sometimes led them to say some unhelpful things about James. We've already seen Martin Luther's view of James. While he didn't rank it highly, he never dismissed its usefulness. He was too committed to the historic Christian faith to make that kind of move. Though he also accepted James as canonical and granted that nothing in the letter is antithetical to Scripture, even John Calvin stated that it was "more sparing in proclaiming the grace of Christ than it behooved an Apostle to be."[12]

Even though they may not have been completely fair to James, both Luther and Calvin consistently taught that faith and works were necessary parts of the Christian life. As the Reformers wrote new documents like the Helvetic Confessions to summarize the key doctrines of the Christian faith, they included statements emphasizing that saving faith must produce good works.

The English Reformers shared this understanding, which they expressed in the Thirty-nine Articles of Religion of the Church of England in 1563. In articles 11–12, they explain their understanding of justification and good works. First, they wrote, "We are accounted righteous before God only for the merit of our Lord and Savior Jesus Christ by faith, and not for our own works or deservings." But this righteous status does not remain alone: "Albeit that good works, which are the fruits of faith, and follow after justification . . . are they pleasing and acceptable to God in Christ, and do spring out necessarily of a true and lively faith insomuch that by them a lively faith may be as evidently known as a tree discerned by the fruit."[13]

In the centuries since the Reformation, Christians have asked many questions about the relationship between justification and good works. However, faithful Protestants have always affirmed that faith and works are distinct but ultimately inseparable and absolutely necessary for true followers of Jesus. More recently, American evangelicals have had dust-ups over things like the role of repentance and allegiance to Jesus in saving faith and the need to preach and teach that good works are the necessary fruit of salvation.

If we have a good handle on the complementary way James and Paul talk about faith and works, we cannot deny the necessity of faith-fueled good works. If we are going to learn from the church through the centuries, we must teach clearly that ongoing faithfulness is not optional. Yes, we are declared righteous through faith alone. The Protestant Reformation helped clarify this truth. We will not be perfect. However, if we are not growing in holiness, we do not have real saving faith. Yes, we might think we have the status "justified" through faith in Jesus. However, if that status is not fulfilled by our actual Holy Spirit–empowered obedience, then our faith was never true saving faith at all.

Teaching on Justification

We've seen that Scripture, the "Great Tradition" of the Christian church, and the Protestant Reformers all affirm the understanding of faith and works we saw in James and Paul. As we wrap up this overview, I want to adapt Michael Bird's helpful summary of justification from our last chapter, condensing his list of five down to four.

As we walk through these four categories, we will make some observations about how these should affect our teaching and preaching. From this, in our last chapter, we will apply this understanding of faith, works, and justification to two pressing contemporary questions.

1. Justification Is Forensic and Eschatological

I'm going to combine Bird's first two categories because they actually are two sides of the same coin. We have talked several times about the forensic nature of justification. When we are justified, God declares that we are righteous in His "courtroom" on the final day of judgment. If we are united by faith to Christ, we share in His status as righteous and holy before God. Because of our union with Jesus, His own righteousness is counted as our own. God can justify us right now because He has brought that verdict and declaration from the end of history into the present.

Because of the forensic nature of justification, we can teach about justification in a way that gives people comfort and hope. If we have faith in God's promises through Jesus, our righteous status is secure. We don't need to live in fear that God will somehow reject us or that we won't measure up. We can rest in the confidence that our justification is as sure as Jesus' own righteousness. This is extremely freeing. When we have faith in Christ, we can live with confidence that God is for us and that He will keep us. When His declaration from the end of history has been brought into the present, we can have confidence that all God's promises for us in Jesus really are right and true—and really do belong to us.

The eschatological nature of justification reminds us that we are also living in the age of new-covenant fulfillment. Both James and Paul emphasize that we live in the days that the Old Testament prophets were longing to see, when God would pour out His Spirit on His people. This too should be encouraging for God's people to hear. As Ben Gladd and Matt Harmon conclude, "Through our identification with Jesus Christ by faith, we have begun to experience the promised blessings of the new covenant. Foremost among these blessings is the gift of the Holy Spirit dwelling in us to empower us to obey God."[14] As we experience the new-covenant blessings of justification, we also have the new-covenant gift of the Spirit, who empowers our ongoing obedience.

2. Justification Is Effective

Greg Beale, one of my professors from graduate school, helpfully illustrates the relationship between justification and sanctification with a Costco membership.[15] My wife and I love to shop at Costco. We have four sons and one seminary student living in our house, so this is usually the only place we can find quantities big enough for our household. To shop at Costco, you have to be a member there. When I walk into the store, I have to show the greeter by the front door my membership card. But is the card really the reason I am allowed to shop there? It is a necessary condition for me to get into the store, right? However, it is not the *actual* reason they let me in. They let me shop at Costco because we pay the annual fee—in our case, for the executive membership (yes, we spend enough there to make it worth it).

My Costco membership card is kind of like sanctification and good works. It is necessary to shop at Costco, but it is not the reason I'm allowed to shop there. The membership card is a *necessary condition*, but it is not the ultimate reason I'm allowed into the store. Instead, it is the necessary evidence that I'm allowed in. The ultimate reason they let me in is that I've paid my membership fee.

Justification through faith alone on the basis of my union with Christ is like my actual membership fee. It is not only necessary for me to shop there, it is the actual reason that I can shop there. The membership fee is what we might call a *causal condition*. It is both a condition and a cause.

In many ways, this is the main point of this book. When we say that justification is effective, we mean that justification is inseparable from sanctification and good works. On the one hand, the Bible and most Christians throughout history have recognized that justification and sanctification are two distinct realities. Justification is God's declaration of our righteous status. Sanctification is the actual transformation of our character that is reflected in our faith-fueled good works. But, on the other hand, justification and sanctification are ultimately inseparable, like light and heat. They are both rooted in our real spiritual union with Christ, so that we receive His status (justification) and then are made into His image (sanctification).

As we teach about faith and works, we have to hold this tension together. We have strong biblical reasons to distinguish what we call "justification" and "sanctification." We are declared righteous, and then we become righteous. We have to be equally clear that these two realities cannot truly be separated. Not only is no one saved apart from being declared righteous in Christ through faith, but also no one is saved apart from good works that flow from and fulfill that righteous status. Justification is completely free, faith is a gift, and our good works do not save us. Yet sanctification is inevitable for a Christian, because God has prepared us for good works (Eph. 2:10), and, if I can move outside of James and Paul for just a moment, there is a holiness without which no one will see the Lord (Heb. 12:14).

I admit that this tension is sometimes confusing. We are saved by faith without works, but without works, we will not be saved. But if we can keep in mind this distinction between necessary conditions (my Costco card) and necessary, causal conditions (my Costco member fee), then we will keep faith and works in their proper place in our teaching and preaching.

3. Justification Is Covenantal

When a person is justified, he or she is declared righteous in God's courtroom. We've also seen that when someone is justified, he or she also becomes a full-fledged member of God's covenant people (Gal. 2). Everyone who is justified shares in all the promises of God to Abraham and his offspring, and these promises find their culmination in Jesus, the true Son of Abraham.

One of the important implications of this covenantal aspect of justification for teaching and preaching is that whenever we put up extra barriers to being fully included in God's people, we are confusing or outright denying justification by faith alone. The false teachers in Galatians said that to enjoy all the benefits of being part of God's covenant people, the Gentile Christians had to be circumcised like Jews under the Law. They were saying that to be a part of the new covenant, which fulfills God's covenant with Abraham, then the Gentile Christians had to have faith *and* be circumcised. When they required circumcision to be a part of God's people, they were denying justification by faith alone. We need to be clear whenever we are teaching about faith and works that there are no kinds of good works or earthly statuses that will win us a seat at the table in God's covenant family. We are welcomed into God's covenant people because we are justified by faith alone.

4. Justification Is Trinitarian

Finally, in all of this, we need to remember and proclaim that justification is the work of our triune God. We have not focused much on the doctrine of the Trinity in this book, but just beneath the surface of everything we've seen is a robust trinitarian theology.

Justification is God the Father's declaration that we are righteous before Him and therefore admitted to His people. We are declared righteous because we are united by faith to Jesus, who lived a perfectly faithful life that we could not live and died the death that we deserved. Because of this union with Him, His righteousness is counted as our own and our sin is counted to Him. This union also guarantees that we will be transformed into His image. To ensure this, the Holy Spirit is poured out on us and does a sanctifying work in our heart. As we teach on justification, faith, and works, we must always proclaim that salvation, from beginning to end, is of the Lord. When we see the trinitarian foundation of our justification, this should give us great confidence and joy in what the Father, Son, and Holy Spirit has done to rescue us from our sin. All to the praise of the glory of His grace (Eph. 1:12)!

If we consistently highlight these key concepts in our teaching and preaching from James and Paul, then we will be on solid ground for making good application as we meet different challenges to this understanding of faith and works. Even though there may be some Christians who teach that works are necessary to win God's favor or that good works are completely unnecessary for our final salvation, these errors are easy to identify if we hear someone outright denying the truth. But more often, challenges to James's and Paul's teachings on faith and works that we'll face can be a little more slippery. To help us think about how we should address these, in our last chapter, we will consider two on-the-ground realities: racial reconciliation and same-sex marriage. As we walk through these modern challenges and think together about what we've learned about faith and works, we will be better equipped to respond to these issues more faithfully and see more clearly why these issues really matter.

Chapter 11

FAITH AND WORKS IN REAL LIFE

In this last chapter, I want to move in a direction that might surprise you. We've been swimming in the depths of faith and works in James and Paul in theology and history, but now we are returning to the present. Before we conclude our study, I want us to see how the complementary teachings of James and Paul on faith and works affect some of the modern church's most pressing questions.

When I was planning this chapter, I thought about playing it safe and finishing the book with some generic statements like, "Don't teach works-righteousness by requiring people to keep man-made laws," and "Don't say that Christians can be true followers of Jesus without actually obeying Him." Those are right and true, but I want to get more specific and maybe a little more controversial. At the risk of this blowing up in my face, I want us to consider two specific questions that many people I know are asking. Because, if we are being honest, it is easy for us to sit in our living room Bible study or Sunday school classrooms and talk about biblical principles we want to live out more faithfully. We can talk in our small group about how we need to be more patient, but it becomes a lot harder when we encounter tough and confusing situations.

In the same way, it is easy for me to agree that everyone who is justified by faith alone will demonstrate their status by their good works when I'm sitting in a coffee shop reading theology, but it is a lot harder to move from theological concepts and even pastoral truth to on-the-ground, concrete reality. We hope that we will rise to the occasion like James and Paul did when biblical truth about faith and works is challenged, and we should plan for this. But a great moral philosopher named Mike Tyson once said, "Everybody has a plan until they get punched in the mouth." How will we respond when our commitment to faith and works gets punched in the mouth by cultural pressure and our own sinfulness?

At this point, I may have annoyed some Protestants by insisting on the need for good works. I know if I have any Roman Catholic friends reading this, they probably aren't happy with how I treated the Council of Trent in the last chapter. Lest anyone walk away unhappy, let's talk about how James's and Paul's teachings on justification, faith, and works should shape our view of racism and same-sex marriage.

You might be wondering what these issues have to do with faith and works. Racism in the church is often a subtle denial of justification by faith alone. Any time someone demands more than faith in Jesus alone in order to be declared right with God or to be a full, equal member of His new-covenant community, justification by faith alone is denied. Yet justifying faith cannot remain alone. It requires transformation and good works. This means we cannot affirm same-sex marriage—or any other same-sex romantic relationship—without undermining the need for good works that flow from our faith. I hope you'll see that these issues, and others like them, are where the rubber really hits the road in what James and Paul have taught us. If we do not hold faith and works in their proper place in light of Jesus' new-covenant work when we encounter these kinds of practical issues, we could lose sight of the truth of the gospel.

Same-Sex Marriage

I get the sense that many Christians are unsure about how the church should respond to the legalization of same-sex marriage. I'll confess that I don't have all the answers on this topic, so I want to be careful in what all I say and how I say it. However, I also need to be as clear as I can be. The church certainly needs to do better at caring for people who face same-sex attraction, but I can't see any faithful reading of Scripture that allows same-sex marriage. In fact, to allow this actually violates James's teaching about faith and works.

We've seen over and again that "faith apart from works is dead" (James 2:26). James says if we claim to have faith in Jesus to be justified but don't actually live out that righteous status, then our faith is fake. We are not really justified at all, and our so-called "faith" does not benefit us. James applies this principle by condemning favoritism toward rich people while neglecting the needs of the poor in the church. If we consistently ignore our brothers and sisters in need, then we have not been justified. But this is not the only application we can make. James shows the connection between faith and works in the Old Testament when Abraham went to sacrifice Isaac. We demonstrate our true faith not just by caring for the poor, but with many different kinds of Christian obedience.

So far, so good. All orthodox Christians would say that good works are somehow a necessary part of being a true Christian, even if they disagree about some of the nuances of how I'm interpreting James 2. I would guess that everyone who claims to follow Jesus but also says same-sex marriage is okay would say something similar. In fact, I think many advocates of same-sex marriage understand the necessary connection between their faith and their jobs, money, or politics very well. But, sadly, these advocates of same-sex marriage also separate the necessary connection between faith and works in the same way as James's opponents who separated the necessary connection between faith and caring for the poor.

Some Christians say we can agree to disagree on same-sex marriage, and to do so is not a big deal. I've heard some defend this by saying that we can divide orthodoxy (what we teach) and orthopraxy (what we do). To be clear, the New Testament does have categories for what are often called "disputable matters." Some Christians will say it is right to drink alcohol, while others might say it is wrong or against their conscience. One brother or sister might be fine watching certain TV programs, while others might think watching such is wrong.

A growing number of Christians argue that the marriage question falls in the same category. Some Christians might say same-sex marriage violates God's design for marriage, and others might say it is a valid expression of God's design for marriage. As long as we all can say the Apostle's Creed together, then our disagreement over same-sex marriage is not a big deal, right? After all, in Romans 14:1, Paul commands the church in Rome to accept one another and "not to quarrel over opinions." James does not have quite the same category, but he also recognizes that there are some decisions about how to live that require wisdom (James 4:13–17).

The problem is not every moral issue is a disputable matter. In fact, most aspects of Christian living are pretty clear. Paul would never say that theft is okay for some Christians but not for others. James would never say caring for the poor is a matter of opinion. And neither one would admit that differences about sexuality and marriage fall into the category of "opinions." The consistent witness of both the Old and New Testaments, as well as the consistent witness of the church for two millennia, is that homosexual acts are wrong, regardless of whether they take place within a committed relationship.[1]

I won't lay out a comprehensive biblical argument for traditional marriage here, but there is a consistency to the Bible's teaching on marriage that is much deeper than a series of proof texts. At the very beginning, Genesis 1–2 is clear. God designed marriage to be between a man and a woman (see Gen. 1:26–27). The rest of the Bible bears this out with no wiggle room. Some people say that the commands against same-sex sexual activity in the Mosaic Law (for example, Lev. 20:13) were arbitrary or limited to Israel under the Law. We can say same-sex marriage is wrong, but if we are being consistent, we have to say that mixed fabrics and sowing two kinds of seed in one field are also wrong (Lev. 19:19).

This isn't a book about the Old Testament Law, so we can't get too far into the weeds. But one of the problems with this argument is that the commands against homosexuality are rooted in God's design in marriage and consistent with the rest of the Bible. When considering how to apply a command from the Law, it is helpful to ask whether this command is repeated in other places outside of the Law. Unlike the threads of mixed fabrics, the thread of God's purposes in marriage runs throughout all Scripture. To say otherwise is to fail to see both the way the Bible fits together and God's deeper purposes for marriage.

God's plan for marriage is also reflected in the Old Testament prophets as they called Israel back to covenant loyalty. The vivid example of Hosea's love for his prostitute wife, Gomer, in the Minor Prophets instructs us more about how marriage between a man and a woman reflects the covenant between God and Israel. The marriage covenant was designed to reflect the complementary love between God and His people, and to the degree that we alter this picture, we misunderstand the relationship between God and His covenant people.

This same pattern continues in the New Testament. While it is true that the Gospels never record Jesus specifically addressing homosexuality, He affirms the view of marriage that we see throughout the Bible (see Matt. 19:3–12). It would have been unthinkable for a first-century Jewish teacher to affirm that same-sex relationships were acceptable.

James does not explicitly mention marriage, but when we look at Paul's letters, he shares this perspective with the rest of Scripture and helps clarify the theological foundations of marriage. Paul's argument about the nature of marriage in Ephesians 5:21–33 confirms and expands our understanding of Genesis 1. God designed marriage to symbolize the love between the Messiah Jesus and His bride, the church. To say that same-sex marriage can somehow conform to this picture is a major distortion of the relationship between God and His people. To have two husbands or two wives is like having trying to have two Christs or two churches. It just does not make sense. Paul is also clear about the nature of same-sex sexual activity in Romans 1:26–27, explaining that when people reject God's revelation of His power and authority, they turn to worship the creation. This leads to all kinds of sin, including homosexuality.

Some modern interpreters say that Paul is not really condemning people who commit homosexual acts in Romans 1. Instead, he is saying that the problem comes when heterosexuals go against their nature and have sex with people of the same gender or participate in abusive homosexual acts. In the rest of the Bible, however, including Paul's own teaching in 1 Corinthians 6, all homosexual acts are condemned. There he writes that the unrighteous do not inherit the kingdom of God, and then defines unrighteousness with a number of sins, including idolatry, adultery, theft, greed, drunkenness, and homosexual acts (1 Cor. 6:9–10).[2]

Paul is saying that those who continue in sins like homosexuality without repenting and fighting against them will not inherit the kingdom of God. This is another way of saying that faith without works is dead. If our lives are not actually transformed—notice I did not say perfect—then we have not really been justified. The good news is that in the next verse, Paul reminds the Corinthians (and us) that we were washed, sanctified, and justified through Christ (1 Cor. 6:11). Everyone who is truly united to Jesus will be transformed by Jesus, and that includes turning away from both heterosexual and homosexual immorality.

It's important to note that these warnings apply any time we misuse God's gift of sex, which is intended for the context of marriage between one man and one woman. If we are allowing unrepentant pornography use, repeated infidelity, or casual divorce while opposing same-sex marriage, then we are undermining God's purposes for marriage and are also in danger of condemnation. A biblical sexual ethic means much more than standing against same-sex marriage, but it certainly doesn't mean less than this. We must affirm the goodness of God's purposes of marriage and sex, oppose all the ways we distort this picture, and be quick to repent when we do. And the good news is that when we repent of our sins and trust in Christ, we are united to Him, declared righteous, and have been given the Spirit who helps us fight our sin. We can have joyful confidence that He will give us help to fight against our sins and demonstrate our true union with Him.

Faith without Works

If we begin to teach that faith without Spirit-driven good works is impossible, then we must also teach that same-sex marriage is wrong. Everyone who claims to follow Jesus but says same-sex marriage is allowed puts themselves (along with anyone who listens to them) in danger of having a false faith. They are teaching that it is no big deal to have faith without appropriate obedience (good works). That kind of faith is phony and has no place in the kingdom of God.

Let's be honest, the church has and will get many issues wrong. Whenever we find these, we should be quick to repent of them and turn back to a more faithful path. However, one of the unique marks of the earliest Christians was their distinct view of human sexuality. Unlike most people in the Roman Empire, they rejected sexual immorality of all kinds and refused to compromise on this issue. From its earliest days, the church of Jesus Christ has affirmed that sex between a husband and wife is a good and beautiful thing but that all other forms of sexual activity are sinful. If a person involved in unrepentant homosexual activity entered the first-century Jerusalem church, James would respond to that person the same way he did to the person who neglected to care for the poor: "As the body apart from the spirit is dead, so also faith apart from works is dead" (James 2:26).

Racism

Same-sex marriage is not the only issue to which the contemporary church has failed to properly apply James's and Paul's teachings on faith and works. In recent years, race relations have surged back into the national conversation in America. Even though the race question is unique in America, there are many conversations about race and ethnicity springing up throughout the Western world. If you have tracked the evangelical Christian response to these conversations, you've seen a range of reactions. Depending on the various responses and my mood at the moment, I've been encouraged, surprised, angered, deflated, and outright perplexed by many of these reactions. I'm encouraged and surprised by the number of prominent Christians leaders who have spoken up for our ongoing need for repentance and racial reconciliation. I'm also angered, deflated, and sometimes perplexed by others who claim that the desire for racial reconciliation is motivated by some progressive agenda or a vaguely defined "cultural Marxism."

The answer to the problem of racism in the church and in Western culture is not simple, so I recognize that faithful brothers and sisters could have legitimate disagreements about some aspects of this issue and how best to address it. As I mentioned in our discussion of marriage, I don't pretend to know all of the answers. But I've seen a number of explicit or implicit claims that deny the link between this conversation and the gospel. Some say that racial reconciliation is a social issue, not a gospel issue, and we need to stop talking about race and start talking about the gospel. What some of those responses fail to see is that any time racism is taught or tolerated in the church, it is a kind of works-righteousness that distorts the gospel. To put it in tweet form, racism is a gospel issue.

Jesus + Law = No Gospel

In a certain way, all sin is a threat to the gospel. When I lose my temper with one of my sons and respond to him in a sinful way, it obscures the nature of God as his Father and the transforming power of the gospel in me. Every time I fail to love my wife as Christ loves the church, I fail to display the gospel in my marriage. If I covet a friend's wealth or success or possessions, it undermines my identity and security in Christ alone.

Why, then, is racism in the church a unique threat to the gospel? In short, it demands something other than Jesus to be a full-fledged member of God's people. Whether it is circumcision, a certain code of conduct, or a particular racial, ethnic, or social status, whenever we add a requirement to being an equal part of God's people, we are denying justification by faith alone. We can see this principle most clearly in Galatians 2. We saw earlier in this passage that Paul confronts Peter in Antioch because his behavior "was not in step with the truth of the gospel" (Gal. 2:14). Peter had been eating with Gentile Christians, but when some influential people from Jerusalem came to Antioch, he stopped eating with them. When he did this, he was saying that Jews and Gentiles in the church were not equal members of God's people.

We have plenty of evidence from the first century about the way devout Jews felt about eating with Gentiles. For example, the Jewish book of Jubilees, which was written sometime around 100 BC or earlier, says, "Separate yourself from the Gentiles, and do not eat with them, and do not perform deeds like theirs. And do not become associates of theirs. Because their deeds are defiled, and all their ways are contaminated, and despicable, and abominable."[3]

Back in Galatians 2, when those guys from Jerusalem arrived in Antioch, Peter stopped eating with the Gentile Christians (Gal. 2:12). When he ate with them he was affirming that they were full-fledged members of God's covenant people. The problem was, they were not circumcised. Peter was essentially saying that they did not have to keep the Law and be circumcised to become members of God's new-covenant people. But the men from Jerusalem responded, "Not so fast. We are happy for these Gentiles to turn to the true God in faith and repentance, but to really be part of His people, then they need to keep the law. Once they become real Jews, then you can eat with them."

Because of this, Peter, Barnabas, and several others stopped eating with Gentiles until they were willing to become full-fledged, Law-keeping members of Israel. Paul insists that Peter was out of step with the truth of the gospel because he was forcing the Gentiles to live like Jews to be accepted on equal terms (Gal. 2:14–15). Peter was creating two classes of Christians: full-fledged circumcised Christians and second-tier, uncircumcised Christians. This was a denial of the truth of justification by faith because it was requiring something else beyond Jesus to be fully accepted by God and fully included in His people.

To demand that anyone keep the Law to be a full member of God's people obscures the gospel of grace. This is a form of righteousness by works. It proclaims that Jesus and our Law-keeping, not Jesus alone, makes us full-fledged members of God's people, and it is a false gospel.

Jesus + Anything = No Gospel

Here is where it gets a little more complicated. The Jerusalem guys were not just demanding that the Gentile Christians keep the Law because they thought God's grace was not enough. They also thought that full membership in God's people was only reserved for people who had a particular cultural and, in this case, ethnic identity: Jewish Law-keepers.

Adding to God's free grace and demanding a particular cultural or racial identity are two sides of the same coin. In the Reformed evangelical world that I'm part of, we are quick to condemn anyone who obscures the gospel of grace by saying good works are necessary to be justified. But many of us often unintentionally do the same by explicitly or implicitly demanding cultural homogeneity.

I understand that the modern conception of "race" is a relatively recent innovation. This does not keep it being present in the church and obscuring the gospel, often in ways we fail to recognize. I suspect that many people will object, saying something like, "I would never exclude someone from my church on the basis of race!" or, "I am quick to shut down any racist talk if I hear it in my church!" We need to keep doing this, but we also need to be more aware of subtle structures that create barriers that I, as a white Christian in a majority white church, don't often think about.

For example, in 1948, Martin Luther King Jr. graduated from Morehouse College and was looking for a seminary to attend. He ended up at Crozer Theological Seminary in Pennsylvania, where he learned unorthodox theological views. I don't know if he applied to any other schools, but many of the schools that I would recommend today would not have accepted King as a degree student. Westminster Theological Seminary in Philadelphia did not graduate their first African American student for another two years in 1950. My own MDiv alma mater, the Southern Baptist Theological Seminary, had launched a "Negro Extension" department around 1940, but would not admit African Americans as regular students until 1951. Because of the color of his skin, King could not have gone to these seminaries as a regular student. I don't know that he ever considered these schools, but if he did, he would not have been accepted in the same way a white man from Georgia would have been. To be admitted to these seminaries, students were required to have Jesus and a certain racial identity, and it was an offense to the gospel.

We might say, "Yes, this is a tragedy, but thank God that this does not happen anymore." Amen. Praise God, every seminary I know gladly accepts brothers and sisters of every ethnicity and cultural background. In fact, while I was writing this book, Southern Seminary released a full report admitting its complicity in slavery and racial discrimination and calling for ongoing reconciliation.

What about the dynamic in our churches? Do we have any expectations for members, Sunday school teachers, or pastors that are rooted in cultural or racial expectations rather than gospel truth? Consider your own church. What do you expect of your leaders? Are you happy to accept members of any cultural background but slow to give people of other ethnicities positions of influence? When was the last time someone from a different culture or ethnicity than the majority in your congregation preached in a Sunday morning worship service? If it has been a while, why do you think that is? Is it possible that you unintentionally expect people of other ethnicities or cultures to conform to the way the rest of your congregation dresses, talks, and looks before you let him or her on the "inside"? Any of these practices are a demand cultural conformity in addition to faith in Jesus. They are a form of works-righteousness and they obscure the gospel.

Works-righteousness is any attempt to gain a right standing with God by anything apart from Christ. These can be "religious" good works, relying on our family of origin, our career, community status, or ethnicity. Any time we demand something apart from faith and repentance to be a full-fledged member of God's people, we are obscuring the gospel. Any time we implicitly or explicitly demand a cultural or racial identity to be a full-fledged member of our churches or institutions, we are obscuring the gospel. God help us to continue to fight against these sins in our churches and Christian institutions.

Whether we are dealing with racism, same-sex marriage, or any other issue, we need to faithfully apply the whole Bible's teaching on faith and works. The Scriptures are clear that faith alone justifies. The Scriptures are equally clear that faith without works does not save. Racism is a denial of justification by faith alone. Same-sex marriage is a denial of the necessity of good works to be saved. God help us to be faithful in understanding and applying both James's and Paul's teaching on these crucial issues. Our triune God has delivered a people who are transformed by His grace because of their union with Jesus, who enables them to share His status right now by faith alone. Praise God for the great truth of justification by faith alone that does not remain alone.

UNITY, DIVERSITY, AND FAITHFULNESS

So what does the Bible teach about faith and works?

Do you remember our friend from the beginning of this book who insisted that any attempts at good works are a kind of legalism? Or the church lady neighbor who told us that God helps those who help themselves? Neither of these people understand that faith alone is necessary to be united to Jesus, but the necessary fruit of that kind of faith is good works. Like the false teachers that Paul and James were answering, both of them have a wrong view of faith or works.

Our friend who is afraid of legalism does not see that our righteous status must be fulfilled by good works. Faith without works is phony faith. But the church lady is not seeing that works we do to win God's favor are useless works. However, after we are joined to Christ by faith, we are then empowered to truly walk in obedience.

This right understanding of faith and works also helps us answer the college professor who teaches that James and Paul were opposing and contradicting each other. As we saw, their lives and ministries followed a similar path. They were both born into families that sought to be faithful to the Law of Moses, but both also initially failed to see that Jesus was the promised Messiah.

And both of them were transformed when they came face-to-face with the risen Christ. Because of this, they devoted their lives to the same cause: proclaiming the gospel of Jesus Christ.

In this great task, James and Paul labored in different areas, and with those differences came unique challenges for each of them. But their fundamental message was the same. God is keeping His new-covenant promises through Jesus the Messiah. Jesus perfectly fulfilled the Law of Moses, and now calls and equips His followers keep the law of liberty, as James puts it, or the law of Christ, as Paul calls it. Both men agree that faith followed by works is the necessary path for every true follower of Jesus. If I can borrow from what philosopher Alvin Plantinga says about science and religion, there may be a superficial conflict between James and Paul, but when we actually understand them, there is deep concord between them and their teachings on faith and works.[1]

Unity or Diversity?

I don't know if James and Paul enjoyed being together or if they were often on each other's nerves. I don't know if they spent much time together beyond what we see in the New Testament. I don't even know for sure whether they read each other's letters. I suspect they did, but that's not really the point. What we do know is that they were united in their faith in Jesus, in their doctrine, and in their teaching about how we ought to live. As we come to the end of our study, I hope you've seen this unity more clearly.

Sometimes biblical scholars like to talk about unity in diversity in the New Testament. I think this is helpful, as long as we affirm the depth of the unity that James and Paul had (along with Matthew, Luke, Peter, and the rest of the authors of the Bible). Even though we have to allow for different personalities and emphases, the diversity in the Bible is rooted more in different ministry contexts and circumstances than any substantial differences among the apostles. As we saw, James and Paul had different emphases because they had to address different problems. When we apply their shared teaching on faith and works in our own unique settings, we will often have to emphasize one side of the equation or the other.

In the last chapter, I tried to show that racism in the church is often a subtle denial of justification by faith alone. But this is not the only circumstance in which justification by faith alone might be threatened. Any time someone demands more than faith in Jesus alone in order to be declared right with God or to be a full, equal member of His new-covenant community, justification by faith alone is denied. We need to fight it every place we see it. The danger to require more than faith alone to be justified is often a danger in conservative churches. We tend to add rules that the Bible does not. But any rule—like don't drink, don't chew, and don't run with girls who do; racial or economic barriers; or any other standard of behavior or status—requiring anyone to check additional boxes beyond Jesus to be justified is a terrible error that we should oppose with everything in us.

We've also seen over and again that true, justifying faith cannot remain alone. It requires transformation and good works. In the last chapter, I argued that this means we cannot affirm same-sex marriage without undermining the need for good works that flow from our faith. Of course, this is also true about any number of sins that we tolerate. While more progressive churches are often guilty of excusing culturally acceptable sins, many churches throughout history have been guilty of overlooking the need for faithful good works. If we find ourselves overlooking sin or explaining it away, we need to fight against that error on every front as well.

I'll admit that knowing how to apply the unified message

of the Bible to diverse circumstances can be tricky. We must always be clear about the gospel and our response. Jesus died for our sins, rose again, and is seated at the Father's right hand. He is coming again to judge the living and the dead. Everyone who trusts in Him alone is united to Him and will be saved. Everyone who is saved will pursue faithful good works. But it can be difficult to know how to address faith and works in a way that puts each in their proper place. Sometimes we need to push people toward greater Spirit-driven labor toward faithful good works. Other times, we need to encourage people to rest in Jesus' finished work for us. And sometimes, we just aren't sure what to say. When we move through our lives at home, at school, in our offices, and in the coffee shop, we need wisdom from God to understand and apply these doctrines faithfully.

Wisdom from Above

In the first chapter of his letter, James writes, "If any of you lacks wisdom, let him ask God, who gives generously to all without reproach, and it will be given him" (James 1:5). Teaching, preaching, and living out the Bible's teaching about faith and works requires wisdom. We need wisdom to know our own hearts well enough to understand whether we are tempted toward earning our standing with God (justification by works) or whether we are inclined toward ignoring our growth in holiness (faith without works). We also need wisdom to help others see the same in their own hearts. And we need wisdom to be able to diagnose whether our families, churches, and other institutions are inclined toward one ditch or the other. But the good news is that God loves to give His wisdom to His children!

As we seek wisdom from the Lord, we need to learn from the whole Bible. Paul's letters help us see the error of seeking justification by works, but they do not ignore the need for good works that flow from this justification. James teaches that faith without works is dead, but this does not mean he ignores faith. He helps us see what true saving faith really looks like. Both of these apostles point us back to Abraham's faith in Genesis so that we see that their shared message about faith and works is found in the whole Bible. The people of God have always been justified by faith alone, but this faith could never remain alone.

Holding these complementary truths together has been challenging for Christians throughout the centuries. We can easily end up in the ditch of works-righteousness, as many late medieval Roman Catholics did, or in the ditch of faith without works, as many in modern evangelicalism do. But when God's people have had the wisdom to return to the truth of the Bible, they've seen that faith followed by works is the calling of all true followers of Jesus.

Let's follow the example of so many Christians who have come before us. Let's hold tenaciously to the truth that we are justified by faith apart from works. Let's proclaim the glory and sufficiency of Christ in salvation. And let's fulfill this righteous status we are given as we pursue love for God and neighbor, as we display God's grace through our labor, giving, and service in our churches, in our neighborhoods, and among all nations.

May God grant us the wisdom to faithfully believe, love, and teach these great complementary truths. God saves us by faith alone, but He does not leave us alone. By His Spirit, we are able to grow in faithfulness and obedience. As Paul wrote in his letter to the Philippians, we are able to work out our own salvation with fear and trembling only because it is God who works in us, both to will and to work for His good pleasure (Phil. 2:12–13). To Him alone be the glory, as it was in the beginning, is now, and will be forever. Amen.

ACKNOWLEDGMENTS

I t is cliché to say that no book can be written alone, but it is true. There are more people to thank (or blame) for this book than I'll likely be able to remember, but I will give it a try.

Thanks to my brothers Todd Morikawa, pastor of Kailua Baptist Church, and Heath Hale, rector at Christ the Foundation Anglican Church in Kailua, Hawaii. Our lunch conversations and text threads have help shape my thinking on faith and works, and your comments on drafts of this book have improved it in many ways. Of course, I'm expecting that neither of you will agree with everything I say, but I'm looking forward to straightening you both out over lunch sometime soon.

I also owe thanks to many others who helped this book come to fruition. My colleagues in the St. John Fellowship of the Center for Pastoral Theologians provided helpful feedback as I first started this project. Thanks as well to my colleagues at Bethlehem College & Seminary, who have provided helpful input in many informal conversations along the way. Doug Moo provided initial input on the structure of the book and agreed to write a foreword. David Griffiths read the whole manuscript and helped sharpen it in several ways. Several other friends provided valuable feedback on the manuscript: Christian Siania, Scott Dunford, Jonathan Arnold, Daniel Patz, Mark Lanier, John Piper, and Brian Tabb. My fellow professors and my students at Bethlehem College &

Seminary, and especially the students in the James and Galatians course, have helped me sharpen my thinking on many of these issues. Drew Dyck, Kevin Emmert, and the team at Moody have been great encouragers along the way and helped improve the book in many ways. Of course, any remaining errors in this book are mine and mine alone.

My wife, Katie, also read the whole manuscript and provided encouragement and feedback, not to mention the unrelenting love and support she always shows me. She and our four sons, Luke, Simon, Elliot, and Noah, have loved and supported me in more ways than I realize.

Sadly, close male friendships have become increasingly rare. In His kindness, God has given me more genuine friendships than most men my age that I know. I've dedicated this book to six of these friends, who are not my pastors but have been faithful shepherds as I've walked through several challenging situations the last few years: Jonathan Arnold, Scott Dunford, David Griffiths, Heath Hale, Todd Morikawa, and Daniel Patz. These brothers have pushed me toward greater faithfulness in every area of my life.

> *For by grace you have been saved through faith. And this is not your own doing; it is the gift of God, not a result of works, so that no one may boast. For we are his workmanship, created in Christ Jesus for good works, which God prepared beforehand, that we should walk in them.*
>
> Ephesians 2:8–10

Soli Deo Gloria
Advent 2018
Burnsville, MN

NOTES

Introduction: Irreconcilable Differences?

1. Martin Luther, *Luther's Works, vol. 35: Word and Sacrament I*, eds. J. J. Pelikan, H. C. Oswald, and H. T. Lehmann (Philadelphia: Fortress Press), 362.
2. Ibid., 397, n. 54.
3. I am taking the New Testament as straightforward history. I believe that Scripture is inspired by God and so is without error in everything it teaches. When it teaches history, I believe that its history is true and accurate. For a good overview of the reliability of New Testament history, see Craig L. Blomberg, *The Historical Reliability of the New Testament: Countering the Challenges to Evangelical Christian Beliefs*, B&H Studies in Christian Apologetics (Nashville: B&H Academic, 2016).

Chapter 1: James, Brother of Jesus

1. Paul also speaks of the "brothers of the Lord" in 1 Corinthians 9:5 but doesn't identify them by name.
2. Epiphanius, *Panarion* 29.4.2 in *The Panarion of Epiphanius of Salamis: Book I: (sects 1–46)*, 2nd ed., Nag Hammadi and Manichaean Studies 63, trans. Frank Williams (Leiden, Netherlands: Brill, 2009), 125.

Chapter 2: Paul, Persecutor of the Church

1. Not to mention, the word *saulos* in Greek is also an adverb that describes the way that prostitutes walk (see E. Randolph Richards, *Paul and First-Century Letter Writing: Secretaries, Composition and Collection* [Downers Grove, IL: IVP Academic, 2004, 128]). I can see how this could have been a problem in places like Corinth!

Chapter 3: James the Just, Servant of Jesus Christ

1. C. S. Lewis, *The Lion, the Witch and the Wardrobe* (New York: Harper Collins, 1950), 139.

2. Ibid.
3. Eusebius Pamphili, *Ecclesiastical History: Books 1–5*, trans. Roy J. DeFarrari, vol. 19 in *The Heroes of the Church* (Washington, DC: Catholic University Press, 1953), 126.
4. James refers to Jesus as Lord at least seven times (1:1, 7; 2:1; 5:7, 8, 10, 14). Most of these references have a direct reference to His imminent return.
5. Eusebius, *Ecclesiastical History, Books 1–5*, 128.

Chapter 4: Paul, Apostle of Jesus

1. Syncing up the accounts of Paul's life in Acts and Galatians is a perennial puzzle for New Testament scholars. As I did with James, I'm giving my best guess about how to fit all the pieces together while also recognizing that Christians who are smarter and more faithful than I am might do it differently.
2. See, for example, Michael F. Bird, *An Anomalous Jew: Paul among Jews, Greeks, and Romans* (Grand Rapids: Eerdmans, 2016).

Chapter 5: The Shared Ministry of James and Paul

1. C. H. Dodd, *The Apostolic Preaching and Its Developments: Three Lectures* (Chicago: Willet, Clark & Co., 1937), 16.
2. Scholars debate whether Galatians 2:1–10 refers to Paul's visit in Acts 11 or the Jerusalem Council in Acts 15. However, both the chronology in Acts and the details Paul describes in Galatians 2 seem to fit Acts 11 better. Paul says he went up to Jerusalem because of a revelation, which probably refers to Agabus's prophecy (Gal. 2:2; Acts 11:28); the meeting was private, not a public council like we see in Acts 15 (Gal. 2:2), and the focus on caring for the poor in Galatians 2:10 lines up well with the purpose of Paul's visit in Acts 11.
3. See the overview of this collection in Chris Bruno and Matt Dirks, *Churches Partnering Together: Biblical Strategies for Fellowship, Evangelism, and Compassion* (Wheaton, IL: Crossway, 2014), 25–27.
4. This teaching was probably the reason Paul needed to write the letter of Galatians.

Chapter 6: Abraham's Foundational Faith (Gen. 15:6)

1. "Psalms of Salomon," in *A New English Translation of the Septuagint*, Albert Pietersma and Benjamin G. Wright, eds. (New York: Oxford University Press, 2007), 771.
2. Philo of Alexandria, *On Virtues: Introduction, Translation, and Commentary*, trans. Walter T. Wilson, Philo of Alexandria Commentary Series 3 (Leiden, Netherlands: Brill, 2011), 87.
3. As we've seen a couple of times already, Sarah's name was changed along the way. This change is a little more subtle. When we first meet

her, she was called "Sarai," which means something like "my princess."
This was later changed to "Sarah," which probably means "princess of
many."

4. Brian Vickers, *Jesus' Blood and Righteousness: Paul's Theology of Imputation* (Wheaton, IL: Crossway, 2006), 77.

5. For more on these questions, check out Paul Copan, *Is God a Moral Monster? Making Sense of the Old Testament God* (Grand Rapids: Baker, 2011), especially 42–55.

6. The full account is in Philo, *On Virtue*, sections 212–19.

Chapter 7: James, Justification, and Fake Faith (James 2:14–26)

1. For more discussion and a convincing response to this view, see Douglas J. Moo, *The Letter of James*, The Pillar New Testament Commentary (Grand Rapids: Eerdmans, 2000), 121.

2. This confession is typically called the *Shema* after its first word in Hebrew (שְׁמַע), meaning "hear."

3. Rabbi Ibn Ezra argued that Isaac was thirteen years old, and there is a significant Jewish tradition that Isaac was thirty-seven years old in Genesis 22. At the very least, Isaac had to be old enough to carry a bundle of wood for the sacrifice to the top of the mountain (see James Goodman, *But Where Is the Lamb? Imagining the Story of Abraham and Isaac* [New York: Schocken Books, 130–31]).

4. See Eugene H. Peterson, *A Long Obedience in the Same Direction: Discipleship in an Instant Society* (Downers Grove, IL: IVP Books, 2000).

5. Moo, *The Letter of James*, 143.

6. Martin Luther, *Commentary on Romans*, trans. J. Theodore Mueller (Grand Rapids: Kregel Classics, 1976), xvii.

Chapter 8: Paul, Justification, and Godly Good Works (Gal. 3 and Rom. 4)

1. Philo, *De Abrahamo*, 270, in Philo, *On Abraham. On Joseph. On Moses*, trans. F. H. Colson, Loeb Classical Library 289 (Cambridge, MA: Harvard University Press, 1935).

2. Mathetes, *The Epistle to Diognetus*, 9:2–5, in *The Apostolic Fathers*, trans. Michael W. Holmes (Grand Rapids: Baker, 2007), 709–710.

3. Ibid.

Chapter 9: Faith, Works, and Justification

1. Rich Mullins, "Screen Door" (Edward Grant, Inc., 1987).

2. For a thorough summary of the "already and not yet" in the New Testament, see Thomas R. Schreiner and Ardel B. Caneday, *The Race Set*

Before Us: A Biblical Theology of Perseverance & Assurance (Downer's Grove, IL: IVP Academic, 2001), 46–86.

3. If you're looking for an exegetical defense of this doctrine, see Brian Vickers, *Jesus' Blood and Righteousness: Paul's Theology of Imputation* (Wheaton, IL: Crossway, 2006).

4. John Calvin, *The Institutes of the Christian Religion*, ed. John T. McNeill, trans. Ford Lewis Battles, 2 vols. (Philadelphia: Westminster, 1960), 3.16.1.

5. John Piper, *The Future of Justification: A Response to N. T. Wright* (Wheaton, IL: Crossway, 2007), 187.

6. J. I. Packer, *Concise Theology: A Guide to Historic Christian Beliefs* (Carol Stream, IL: Tyndale House, 1993), 164.

7. Michael Bird, "Progressive Reformed View," in *Justification: Five Views*, eds. James K. Beilby and Paul Rhodes Eddy (Downers Grove, IL: IVP Academic, 2011), 156.

Chapter 10: Preaching and Teaching James and Paul through the Centuries

1. If you are interested in studying the history and development of the New Testament canon more, see Michael J. Kruger, *Canon Revisited: Establishing the Origins and Authority of the New Testament Books* (Wheaton, IL: Crossway, 2012).

2. These numbers are based on searches in Accordance Bible Software. Depending on a few textual variants, the numbers could vary, but the point still stands.

3. Cyril of Jerusalem, *Catechetical Lectures* 5.5, cited in ed. Gerald Bray, *James, 1–2 Peter, 1–3 John, Jude*, vol. 11 of *Ancient Christian Commentary on Scripture: New Testament*, ed. Thomas C. Oden (Downers Grove, IL: InterVarsity Press, 2000), 33.

4. Augustine, *On the Christian Life* 13, cited in Bray, *James, 1–2 Peter, 1–3 John, Jude*, 30–31.

5. *Questions* 76.1, cited in ed. Gerald Bray, *Romans*, vol. 6 of *Ancient Christian Commentary on Scripture: New Testament*, ed. Thomas C. Oden (Downers Grove, IL: InterVarsity Press, 1998), 105.

6. Venerable Bede, *Concerning the Epistle of St. James*, cited in Bray, *James, 1–2 Peter, 1–3 John, Jude*, 31.

7. Andreas the Presbyter, *Catena*, cited in Bray, *James, 1–2 Peter, 1–3 John, Jude*, 32.

8. For example, scholars disagree about Augustine's understanding of justification. Some argue that he confused justification and sanctification, but he is not always clear (at least in answering some of the questions we might have). However, to require the same level of clarity from fourth century and sixteenth century theologians is unreasonable.

9. For a helpful overview of the early church's teaching and preaching on justification, see the discussion in Michael Horton, *Justification*, 2 vols.,

New Studies in Dogmatics (Grand Rapids: Zondervan, 2018), 1:39–91. While scholars disagree about the precise understanding of faith and works in the church fathers, Horton is correct to conclude, "*salvation was understood as by grace alone, in Christ alone, through faith rather than works.*" However, for some, "*justification* was understood . . . as synonymous with the entire process of salvation. Hence, the distinct role of justification in the *ordo salutis*—namely, the imputation of Christ's righteousness rather than impartation of inherent righteousness—though not denied, does not seem even to have occurred to these formative theologians of the early medieval era" (1:91).

10. Horton, *Justification*, 1:279.

11. "The Council of Trent," in *A Reformation Reader: Primary Texts with Introductions*, 2nd ed., ed. Denis R. Janz (Minneapolis, MN: Fortress Press, 2008), 408 (emphasis added). Horton is right to conclude that this declaration "severs the real ontological connection between Christ and the believer's salvation" (*Justification*, 1:204).

12. John Calvin, *Commentaries on the Epistle of James*, Calvin's Commentaries (Grand Rapids: Baker Academic, 1999), 276.

13. "The Thirty-nine Articles," in *A Reformation Reader*, 370–71.

14. Benjamin L. Gladd and Matthew S. Harmon, *Making All Things New: Inaugurated Eschatology in the Life of the Church* (Grand Rapids: Baker, 2016), 32.

15. G. K. Beale, "Resurrection in the Already-And-Not-Yet Phases of Justification," in *For the Fame of God's Name: Essays in Honor of John Piper*, eds. Sam Storms and Justin Taylor (Wheaton, IL: Crossway, 2010), 204: "The card is necessary to get into the store, but it is not ultimate reason that the person is granted access. The paid fee is the ultimate reason for the entrance, and the card is the evidence that the fee has been paid. We may refer to the fee paid as the necessary causal condition of entrance into the store and the evidence-testifying card as the necessary condition (but not the necessary causal condition). The card is the external manifestation or proof that the prior price was paid, so that both the money paid and the card are necessary for admittance, but they do not have the same conditional force for allowing entrance."

Chapter 11: Faith and Works in Real Life

1. See Sam Allberry, *Is God Anti-Gay?* (Questions Christians Ask; *n.p.*: The Good Book Company, 2013). To understand the purposes for marriage, gender, and the body more fully, see the arguments in Todd Wilson, *Mere Sexuality: Rediscovering the Christian Vision of Sexuality* (Grand Rapids: Zondervan, 2017); John Paul II, *Man and Woman He Created Them: A Theology of the Body*, trans. Michael M. Waldstein (Boston: Pauline Books, 2006).

2. The word ἀρσενοκοῖται in 1 Corinthians 6:9 is controversial. It is translated "men who practice homosexuality" in the ESV, and most modern English versions are similar. Some have argued that Paul is singling out some homosexual acts but not all. This word is unique, but it is likely

that Paul may have invented a word that combines two words from the Greek OT translation of Leviticus 18:22, which says, "You shall not lie (κοίτην) with a man (ἄρσενος) as with a women" (my translation). In any case, Paul is clearly linking this prohibition to the rest of the Bible's instructions about sexuality.
3. Jubilees 22:16.

Epilogue: Unity, Diversity, and Faithfulness

1. The thesis of Plantinga's book *Where the Conflict Really Lies: Science, Religion, and Naturalism* (Oxford: Oxford University Press, 2011), is: "There is superficial conflict but deep concord between science and theistic religion, but superficial concord and deep conflict between science and naturalism" (ix).

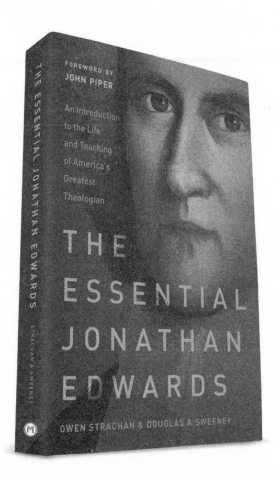

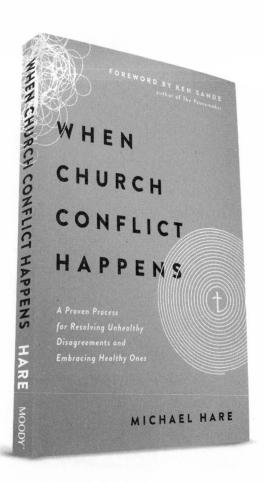